BRINGING INTELLIGENCE ABOUT

Practitioners Reflect on Best Practices

May 2003

Russell G. Swenson, Editor

**With a Foreword by
Mark M. Lowenthal
Assistant Director of Central Intelligence**

The Joint Military Intelligence College supports and encourages research on intelligence that distills lessons and improves support to policy-level and operational consumers, and that familiarizes the public with aspects of the intelligence profession.

Bringing Intelligence About: Practitioners Reflect on Best Practitioners

The title chosen for this book carries two meanings. The more straightforward interpretation of "Bringing Intelligence About," and the principal one, refers to the book's coverage of wide-ranging sources and methods employed to add value to national security-related information—to create "intelligence." A second meaning, not unrelated to the first, refers to the responsible agility expected of U.S. intelligence professionals, to think and act in such a way as to navigate information collection and interpretation duties with a fix on society's shifting but consensual interpretation of the U.S. Constitution.

A prominent individual and ideal intelligence professional who lived both meanings of "Bringing Intelligence About" was the late Lieutenant General Vernon A. Walters. As an intelligence officer, defense attache, ambassador-at-large and ambassador to Germany, his combination of skills—notably his language skills—made him the epitome of a professional. Beyond intelligence service in the Departments of Defense and of State, General Walters presided as Deputy Director of Central Intelligence during the Watergate episode, where he stood on principle and at odds with political figures in the Nixon administration. His mastery of intelligence collection, analysis and politically attuned synthesis, the full story of which has not yet been told, make him a near-mythic figure for aspiring intelligence professionals.

Although the talents and assignments of General Walters were extraordinary, his demonstration that intelligence aptitudes and skills are fungible across Departments and Agencies is a powerful suggestion that those separate institutions can also operate together as a professional community.

The papers in this publication are based exclusively on sources available to the public and the views expressed are those of the respective authors, and do not necessarily reflect the official policy or position of the Department of Homeland Security, the Department of Defense or the U.S. Government.

This publication has been approved for unrestricted distribution by the Office of the Secretary of Defense (Public Affairs). Copies of this publication are available in limited quantities to U.S. Government officials, and to the public through the National Technical Information Service (www.ntis.gov), or the U.S. Government Printing Office (www.gpo.gov).

Russell.Swenson@dia.mil
Editor

FOREWORD

There are two anecdotes from the world of entertainment that seem apt to introduce this book.

First: The great 19th-century Anglo-Irish actor Edmund Kean lay on his deathbed. A friend asked, "Is it hard, Edmund?"

"No," he replied. "Dying is easy. *Comedy* is hard."

Second: A Hollywood producer in the 1930s or 1940s was asked why a certain film succeeded at the box office but another did not. He replied, "If we knew the answer to that, we'd only make hits."

Similarly, the process of intelligence is easy; *good* intelligence is hard. And if we could figure out what made some intelligence "good" or "better" (which would require some further definition), then we would produce it more regularly.

We spend a lot of time in the Intelligence Community analyzing the various parts of the intelligence process and trying to define what makes some intelligence better than other intelligence. And yet, for all that intellectual effort, we still have not evolved a steady and reliable means of producing this "better" intelligence. We know when the process works and when it does not, but this knowledge does not turn into a formula for greater success.

Why is that? Are we unable to learn from our own successes and failures? Or does the process remain so intangible at core that it eludes us even when we have, on occasion, mastered it? My own view is that we have not yet (after more than 55 years) come up with a good picture in our minds—nor have we successfully enunciated—just what a professional intelligence analyst "looks like," and how we train and develop this analyst across his or her entire career—not just at the outset. Interestingly, we do know what the analyst's ethos is, but we remain fuzzy on the necessary professional underpinnings.

This volume helps us move down the long and difficult road of helping identify how to produce good or better intelligence—by which I mean intelligence that is of use to policymakers and is better than other intelligence by being so used. The authors have—across a range of areas of interest—identified some of the practices that work best to produce—or, more aptly, "to bring about"—good intelligence. Note that the preceding sentence said "some of the practices." Few books could expect to identify all of the practices that work and, as the authors of each chapter would undoubtedly concede, there will always be some variables and intangibles at work in intelligence: vagaries of time to perform collection and analysis; the quality of sources; the quality of the analysts; the nature and personality of the policymakers. Still, it is possible to identify the practices that work and the practices that have to be altered over time as conditions change.

I cannot help but think that if we were to take the various observations and recommendations of these chapters and shape them into a coherent program we would be well on our way to producing better intelligence on a more consistent basis. Of course, we would still face the issue of where that program should exist and how it should be imparted because, for all of the improvements we have made in training and developing analysts, we still do this in vertical, agency-dominated stovepipes. We have a variety of courses that seek to train (or inculcate) people into the broader Community aspects of intelligence, but training remains a series of isolated enterprises. Thus, even if we accept the many good ideas in this book, getting them to all of the people who might benefit from them remains typically problematic.

Finally, it is also important to understand that this book focuses on the issue of analysis. I am admittedly prejudiced in my views, but I believe that analysis is the main goal of any intelligence enterprise: putting informed judgments in front of policymakers to help them make decisions. This is not meant to demean clandestine activities in the field, or the designing and operation of collection systems, or any of the other necessary parts of the broader intelligence function. But, at the end of the day, the most consistent service intelligence provides is analysis, whether it is a one-line warning or a detailed estimate. The Infantry likes to call itself "the Queen of Battle." This is how I feel about analysis in the world of intelligence. This book helps analysis remain firmly placed on her throne.

Mark M. Lowenthal
Assistant Director of Central Intelligence for
    Analysis and Production
Vice-Chairman for Evaluation, National Intelligence
    Council

BRINGING INTELLIGENCE ABOUT PRACTITIONERS REFLECT ON BEST PRACTICES

Contents

List of Figures

ABOUT THE AUTHOR

Dr. Russell G. Swenson directs the Center for Strategic Intelligence Research at the Joint Military Intelligence College. His initial exposure to the world of intelligence was as an Air Force linguist in the mid-1960s. He holds undergraduate degrees from the University of Kansas, and graduate degrees in Geography from the University of Wisconsin-Milwaukee. At the JMIC since 1988, he has taught the course on strategic warning from intelligence, as well as thesis research and writing seminars. He also teaches a course on intelligence issues in Latin America. His research interests include the application of analytic methods and the comparative study of intelligence practices, especially in the Western Hemisphere.

INTRODUCTION

Russell G. Swenson
with David T. Moore and Lisa Krizan

This book is the product of studious self-reflection by *currently serving* intelligence professionals, as well as by those who are in a position, with recent experience and continuing contacts, to influence the development of succeeding generations of intelligence personnel. Contributors to this book represent eight of the fourteen organizations that make up the National Foreign Intelligence Community. A positive image of a community of professionals, engaged in public service, and concerned about continuous self-improvement through "best practices," emerges from these pages.

Practitioners anywhere in this Community are professional by any definition of the term. Their work requires extensive education and specialized training, and at their best, personnel exhibit highly innovative approaches to collection and analysis. Differences in focus among the principal Intelligence Community partners are sometimes sharp, but similarities in techniques do exist, particularly at the "working level." Community partners, such as the Central Intelligence Agency (CIA), Defense Intelligence Agency (DIA), the National Security Agency (NSA), and the State Department's Bureau of Intelligence and Research (INR), for example, share responsibilities for national security issues that allow individual collectors, analysts, issue managers and offices to work together on interagency task forces.

However, commonalities may decrease farther afield, for example between the agencies with a strategic focus and those involved in tactical or law-enforcement intelligence. Not the least of these differences is that, with its strategic focus, the Intelligence Community expects to be forward-looking, envisioning future developments and their repercussions, whereas law enforcement intelligence efforts have typically focused on exploiting pattern analysis to link together the extralegal behavior of individuals and organizations with clear and legally acceptable evidence. Some overlap of intelligence applications already occur, especially in the areas of crime and narcotics, where interagency task forces work from both ends of the problem—the predictive and the reactive—so that a facile claim of significant differences between law enforcement and national security intelligence may hold up to scrutiny only in terms of the scale of operations supported rather than professional intelligence techniques employed. [1] We may infer from these observations that the principles of intelligence collection and analysis addressed in this book will apply to intelligence creation in the broadly overlapping cultures of law enforcement and national security intelligence.

---

[1] Two works that document the evolution of criminal or law enforcement intelligence, both in the U.S. and internationally, are 1) *Intelligence 2000: Revising The Basic Elements: A Guide for Intelligence Professionals*, Marilyn Peterson, ed. (n.p.: Law Enforcement Intelligence Unit, California, and International Association of Law Enforcement Intelligence Analysts, 2000), and 2) Don McDowell, *Strategic Intelligence: A Handbook for Practitioners, Managers and Users* (Cooma, NSW, Australia: Istana Enterprises Pty, Ltd, 1998). These books provide evidence of a convergence, in both instructional and professional standards of practice, between law enforcement and national security intelligence.

The concept of a *Community* of professional intelligence collectors and analysts persists, despite the specialized character of much of their work. Further, the National Foreign Intelligence Community does not remain static, as shown by its recent (2001), formal incorporation of the U.S. Coast. The Coast Guard combines its new intelligence focus with its traditional broad responsibilities in law enforcement, in paramilitary operations, and in public safety. As a new, young member, and a bridge between national security and law enforcement spheres, the USCG is in position to help rejuvenate the community by exemplifying the ideal of sharing both information and assessments.

The U.S. Intelligence Community was subject during the 1990s to a congressionally mandated reduction in Intelligence Community personnel levels.[2] This reduction occurred despite numerous small wars and the continuation of international criminal activity during the decade. When dissenters, such as former Director of Central Intelligence James Woolsey, "talked about the proliferators, traffickers, terrorists, and rogue states as the serpents that came in the wake of the slain Soviet dragon, [they were] accused of 'creating threats' to justify an inflated intelligence budget."[3] Even government reports such as that of the United States Commission on National Security (commonly referred to as the Hart-Rudman Report), which warned of catastrophic attacks against the American homeland and a need for vigilance, were dismissed.[4]

Intelligence collectors and analysts have at times been subject to personnel retrenchment, a situation favoring current operations support, and leading to the neglect of individual and corporate succession planning—to capture and pass on institutional and target knowledge. Today, collection and analysis tradecraft remain neglected phenomena—the focus of very few self-studies.[5] Naturally, some literature known to "insiders" is not made available to the general public because of the admonition not to disclose "sources and

---

[2] John E. McLaughlin, CIA Deputy Director of Intelligence, notes that the reduction was 22 percent. See McLaughlin's "The Changing Nature of CIA Analysis in the Post-Soviet World," remarks as prepared for delivery at the Conference on CIA's Analysis of the Soviet Union, 1947-1991, 9-10 March 2001 (Princeton, NJ: Princeton University, 2001), URL: <http://www.cia.gov/cia/public_affairs/speeches/archives/2001/ddci_speech_03092001.html>, accessed 22 December 2002. Cited hereafter as McLaughlin.

[3] McLaughlin.

[4] U.S. Commission on National Security/21st Century, *New World Coming: American Security in the 21st Century*, The Phase I Report on the Emerging Global Security Environment for the First Quarter of the 21st Century, Supporting Research and Analysis (Washington, DC: GPO, 15 September 1999), 49.

[5] The few works that do address intelligence practices in informed detail have become classics, and are widely cited. They include Sherman Kent's *Strategic Intelligence For American World Policy* (Princeton, NJ: Princeton University Press, 1949); Roger Hilsman, *Strategic Intelligence and National Decisions* (Glencoe, IL: The Free Press, 1956); Washington Platt, *Strategic Intelligence Production: Basic Principles* (New York: Frederick A. Praeger, 1957); Bruce D. Berkowitz and Allen E. Goodman, *Strategic Intelligence for American National Security* (Princeton, NJ: Princeton University Press, 1989); Richards J. Heuer, Jr., *Psychology of Intelligence Analysis* (Washington, DC: Center for the Study of Intelligence, 1999) and Lisa Krizan, *Intelligence Essentials for Everyone*, Occasional Paper Number Six (Washington, DC: Joint Military Intelligence College, 1999).

methods." However, even though collection methods are often arcane, methods of analysis are not very esoteric. Analytic methods used by intelligence analysts are readily available to specialists in the academic world.[6] The commonalities that do exist among collectors and analysts across the Community have rarely been noted in intelligence literature. The essays in this book will help fill that gap, and should illuminate for non-specialists the important role of self-reflection among intelligence professionals who remain in government service.

The contributors to this book share an interest in exploring and explaining intelligence collection and analysis practices.

Pauletta Otis, whose work has acquainted her with both the Intelligence Community and academia, outlines from experience the numerous similarities and differences between communities of academics and intelligence professionals. Her reminder that academics tend to be "contrarian" points up the value of academics having continual interaction with intelligence experts, in support of the Community's ideal, "nonmonastic" (not following the party line) approach to issues.

In the next essay, retired Navy Captain George Satterthwaite recounts how persistence and creativity when coupled with serendipity can contribute to gathering unique information that may thereby yield valuable intelligence. By taking advantage of his responsibilities as Defense Attaché to host official U.S. delegations, he gained access to important facilities in India for insight into Indian nuclear and naval capabilities. Intelligence professionals can readily relate to his spirited interaction with bureaucratic and political colleagues in the U.S. Embassy and the host country.

It may now be true that the value of intelligence to consumers is more dependent on the evaluation of information (grappling with mysteries) than on discovering "secrets."[7] If so, then the evaluation of social trends in various regions might best begin with systematic exploitation of authentic or "grass-roots" reporting from newspapers and other mass media. In the third essay, John Turner, senior Middle East and North Africa analyst at the U.S. European Command's Joint Analysis Center, illustrates his facility with exploiting multilingual electronic news media from North Africa. Translation and reporting by the Foreign Broadcast Information Service from such media is selective rather than comprehensive, and selections are not tailored for individual analysts, who are removed from first-hand screening of the sources. Therefore, language capabilities are indispensable for any country's intelligence personnel who seek insights through indigenous mass media. Language capabilities must mirror those tongues used across the electronic media that represent the target entities. Further, as noted in a recent news

---

[6] Many if not most analysts have been exposed, by training or experimentation, to such techniques as link analysis, the Delphi technique, and analysis of competing hypotheses. Morgan D. Jones, former CIA analyst, has distilled the less structured techniques that intelligence analysts may employ in *The Thinker's Toolkit: 14 Powerful Techniques for Problem Solving* (New York: Times Business, Random House, 1995 and 1998).

[7] For an "insider's" comparison of secrets" and "mysteries" see John C. Gannon, CIA Deputy Director for Intelligence, speech before the World Affairs Council, 20 March 1996. URL: *http:// www.cia.gov/cia/public_affairs/speeches/archives/1996/ddi_speech_032096.html.*

report, the U.S. experience is that non-native, academically trained linguists who have lived abroad typically outperform native linguists in intelligence assignments that depend on language ability.[8] Dr. Turner's essay, with its emphasis on his own familiarity with North African news media reporting, illustrates that point.

Stephen Marrin reflects on his experiences as a new CIA analyst as he addresses whether and how formal training programs can impart the specialized knowledge, skills, and abilities necessary for meaningful intelligence analysis. He examines how the customary activity, processes, and organization of intelligence may have contributed to some failed aspects of intelligence prior to the events of 11 September 2001. He then suggests some specific ways to reinvent certain aspects of the national intelligence mission to allow analysts to bring greater persuasiveness to their value-added information.

U.S. Air Force Lieutenant Colonel Tom Garin examines how dignity and self-respect among professionals may be fostered within an intelligence organization. Garin defines the intelligence corporation in terms of a "learning organization" and then applies external standards from the Baldrige National Quality Program to selected intelligence-producing offices within the Defense Intelligence Agency. This benchmarking study not only identifies best practices, but also shows how such professional standards could be used to identify exemplary offices or individuals across the entire Intelligence Community.

Available literature does not yet address the question of what knowledge, skills and abilities are required, from the point of view of front-line managers, to support and sustain the evolution of intelligence tradecraft. David Moore and Lisa Krizan define a graduated set of criteria to calibrate an individual's suitability for an analytic position. Given the current Intelligence Community hiring surge, the set of core competencies they identify for NSA also provides a guide for the larger Intelligence Community to improve the professional stature of its workforce by defining who the analysts of the present and future ought to be.

The last essay reveals how the U.S. Coast Guard, having only recently joined the Intelligence Community, has already adjusted its organizational structure and its personnel system, expanded its participation in multi-agency initiatives, and developed procedures for more effective management of its unique position between civilian and military worlds. These rapid developments, stimulated by membership in the Community of Intelligence professionals, should enable the Coast Guard to anticipate and meet the requirements of both law enforcement and national security intelligence. As a fresh-faced affiliate of the Intelligence Community, the Coast Guard can inject an uncompromised determination to help the community live up to its name.

The essays collected here only begin to illustrate the potential of self-reflective writing by intelligence practitioners. If a communitarian ethos distinguishes intelligence professionals from their more individualistic and self-absorbed brethren in academia, then self-reflection among intelligence practitioners can also easily become a communal good. Tension between a communitarian and individualistic ethos can resolve itself among

---

[8] Susan Schmidt and Allan Lengel, "Help Still Wanted: Arabic Linguists," *Washington Post*, 27 December 2002, A23.

intelligence professionals through the strength of their bureaucratic (Weberian), nonmonastic tradition. The essays in this volume illustrate how, through self-reflection, that tension may be resolved. For example, individual professionals can easily spell out connections among these essays that would quickly move the discussion to a classified realm—into their "culture." That culture is typically characterized by fast-moving events and requirements that preclude introspection about the phenomena of intelligence collection and production.

Self-reflection not only allows the various agency sub-cultures to be displayed, as portrayed here, but also allows "insiders" to realize the subtle connections of their individual work to the overall enterprise. As a further illustration of this principle, the intense intellectual effort that characterized earlier eras of intelligence production and that continues as a part of the enduring culture, is evoked by the observations of William Millward, a World War II intelligence analyst at the UK's Bletchley Park:

> [Analysis] means reviewing the known facts, sorting out significant from insignificant, assessing them severally and jointly, and arriving at a conclusion by the exercise of judgment: part induction, part deduction. Absolute intellectual honesty is essential. The process must not be muddied by emotion or prejudice, nor by a desire to please.[9]

National intelligence collection management and intelligence analysis remain inherently government functions, and privatized intelligence—with its prospect of reduced congressional oversight—is even more antagonistic to the communal sharing of information than are the more stringently overseen bureaucratic fiefdoms.[10] In this environment, to "bring intelligence about" from the point of view of the American people requires peeling back some of the thick mantle of secrecy that has shrouded individual initiatives and management approaches—Community best practices—employed in the execution of ordinary and extraordinary tasks. Readers who look closely at the observations set down by the authors here will find a serviceable tool for unwrapping some of the otherwise enigmatic enthusiasms and motivations of government intelligence professionals.

---

[9] William Millward, "Life in and out of Hut 3," in F.H. Hinsley and Alan Stripp, *Codebreakers: The Inside Story of Bletchley Park* (Oxford, UK: Oxford University Press, 1993), 17.

[10] Across the Intelligence Community, the proportion of private, "contract" employees of all categories now stands at about 30 percent, and is growing. Few of these individuals are "independent" contractors, the great majority being associated with small or large private enterprises. Although most such contractors hold high-level security clearances based upon background investigations, the proprietary interests of their "parent" organizations can be at odds with an ethos of uninhibited sharing of information and perspectives. For an exploration of these issues, see James R. Sutton, *Subversion of a Government Monopoly: The Privatization of Intelligence Services* (n.p.: Research Intelligence Consortium, Inc., 2000). For information about the author, see http://www.trinitydc.edu/academics/depts/ Interdisc/International/Jim_Sutton.htm.

ABOUT THE AUTHOR

Pauletta Otis is Professor of Political Science and International Studies at the University of Southern Colorado. Her Ph.D. was awarded from the Graduate School of International Studies at the University of Denver in 1989. Dr. Otis held the position of Distinguished Visiting Professor of International Security Studies at the Joint Military Intelligence College in 1998 and then was Visiting Scholar for the National Security Education Program 1999, under the auspices of the National Defense University. She continues to teach summer sessions at JMIC and contributes to a number of defense research efforts. Dr. Otis maintains an active speaking schedule and has been guest speaker at a number of prestigious meetings including those held by the National War College, National Intelligence Council, Defense Intelligence Agency, Central Intelligence Agency, National Security Agency, U.S. Marine Corps, the Denver Committee on Foreign Relations, and other private and public venues.

Dr. Otis has special expertise in the study of sub-national violence and combines theoretical (from graduate degrees in Anthropology, Political Science, and International Studies) with operational experience and expertise. She has conducted field research in conflict situations in South Asia, Latin America, the Middle East, and the eastern Mediterranean.

THE INTELLIGENCE PRO AND THE PROFESSOR: TOWARD AN ALCHEMY OF APPLIED ARTS AND SCIENCES

Pauletta Otis

Recent events have led to an increasing realization that all of the resources of the American public must be engaged in support of national security. The U.S. academic community and the U.S. National Foreign Intelligence Community are institutional managers of "information as power." Yet their potential for useful cooperation and collaboration is unrealized and the relationship between the communities continues to be somewhat strained. This relationship has been the topic of discussions for many years in a somewhat benign security environment. With dramatic changes in that environment in late 2001, maximizing resources through enhanced cooperation and collaboration assumes critical importance. How can the Intelligence Community (IC) and the academic community best cooperate in support of national security? What are the inherent risks and challenges?

The theoretical challenge is of primary concern. Basic assumptions about the nature of democracy and the nature of secrecy are foundational to each of the communities' view of itself and of the other. The major theoretical concern for both intelligence and academic communities is the apparent contradiction between secrecy and democratic governance. From the academic's point of view, the U.S. Government's stability and its concern for the common welfare derive from the First Amendment. If a stable democracy depends on an informed public, the public cannot make good decisions without accurate and timely information. Without the "self-correcting" mechanism of free speech, a government tends to be subject to centrifugal forces, to spin on its own axis, and to become an entity quite separate from the citizenry.

Yet, on a practical level, we need to "keep secrets" from U.S. enemies, however they may be defined. A certain level of secrecy is required to protect national interests. How much secrecy is "best" in a democracy is subject to ongoing debate.[11] The pendulum swings over time and in response to perceived threats to national security. Subsequent to 11 September 2001, an acceptance of "more secrecy" has accompanied public support for the IC's enhanced role in homeland security. It may also be assumed that eventually a public reaction to perceptions of "too much" secrecy will move the pendulum back toward an historical center. Compromise between requirements to keep secrets must be balanced with the requirements of free speech inherent in the very definition of democracy. CIA Director Stansfield Turner (1977-1981), when he was at the center of the secrecy maelstrom, simply stated: "Accommodating secrecy in a democracy requires compromises with the theory of full freedom of speech, inquiry, and endeavor."[12] The problems inherent to this balancing act

---

[11] Pat M. Holt, *Secret Intelligence and Public Policy: A Dilemma of Democracy* (Washington, DC: CQ Press, 1995), see especially chapter 1.

[12] Stansfield Turner, *Secrecy and Democracy: the CIA in Transition.* Boston, MA: Houghton Mifflin Company, 1985), 112.

have been apparent in all aspects of contemporary American life, yet nowhere so fraught with difficulty as in the relationship between academia and the national security community. This tension, albeit normal, natural, and expected, is often most apparent and most difficult in the relationship between academe and intelligence professionals.[13]

The special caveat is that patriotism is not at issue: degree of commitment to this country is an individual attribute. Whereas the intelligence professional may work on a daily basis with threats to this country, the academic may work on supporting the values and attitudes necessary to sustain democratic life. One focuses on external threat, the other on the internal maintenance of the democratic system itself.

COMMONALITIES

Both the IC and the academic community work in the world of word-power. Both are populated by dedicated and committed Americans. In most cases, cooperative efforts have yielded the "best" for the United States in terms of public policy and decisionmaking. Yet, at other times, the communities have been at serious odds. The ensuing problems have been of significant concern to the attentive public and detrimental to the common good. These problems emanate not only from the theory of democracy but from competition over the nature of truth and value for the country. They can also be traced to concern about the nature and processes of intelligence gathering.

The IC and the academic community have much in common: both realize that information is power and that power comes in the form of words. These words form the basis of cultural assumptions, common concepts, and grand theory. In terms of information handling minutiae, intelligence specialists and academic scholars do much the same thing. They research, write, explain, and predict with excruciating self-consciousness and realization of the power of words. Intelligence professionals and academics contribute to public discussion in both oral forums and in written format. Intelligence professionals and academics are valued and participant citizens: They attend common religious services, participate in the education of children, contribute to community service organizations, and talk to neighbors. At this level, both are truly in the same "game." In the public domain, both intelligence professionals and academics contribute information, analysis, and opinions. These are read and integrated by the public, by policymakers, and by the "other" community. This common body of public information and analysis is at the core of intelligent decisionmaking in the United States.

For 50-plus years, relations between the IC and academia have wavered between cooperation and competition. The basic tension inherent in keeping "secrets in a democracy" has been played out in specific activities and attitudes. These can be seen at the individual, institutional, and political levels. At the individual and institutional levels, no doubt in part because of the strong influence of Ivy League academics in World War II intelligence

---

[13]Robert M. Gates, as CIA Deputy Director for Intelligence in 1986, addressed the John F. Kennedy School of Government at Harvard University on the relationship between the IC and academe. His address was published as "CIA and the University," in *Studies in Intelligence* 30, no. 2 (Summer 1986): 27-36.

(especially in the Office of Strategic Services), considerable rapport between academe and government intelligence was maintained.[14] Universities and study centers were also involved in the ongoing relationship between the intelligence and academic communities. Between 1939 and 1961, Yale University was overtly supportive of the IC.[15] Students and faculty were participants in intelligence collection and analysis. Study centers were financially supported and professional journals published. Information was collected and archived (including the Human Relations Area Files). The money was channeled to individuals or to institutions but seemed to raise few concerns.[16] At the political level, the existence of a "community" of intelligence-related agencies and offices has been noted in legislation, suggesting wide acceptance of the idea of government intelligence operations as regularized institutions with special taskings in support of U.S. national security.[17]

CONTINUITY, CHANGE, AND THE DEVELOPMENT OF DIFFERENCES

The "position descriptions" of an intelligence specialist and of an academic are polar opposites: The basic job of an academic is to find information, collect factoids whether they are useful or not–and scatter the information to the winds hoping and praying to make more sense of the ensuing chaos. Intelligence specialists collect similar factoids for very specific productive purposes. Whereas the academic is spreading information, the intelligence professional is collecting, narrowing, and refining data to produce reports, even if at the same time continuing an academic interest in the subject. The academic may learn for the fun of it; the intelligence professional prefers, or learns to be able to actually *do* something with the information. In the long run, the academic must write, produce, and contribute to the body of professional literature, but there is not the pressure for immediate production that the intelligence professional must face. The academic can say "that is interesting"; the intelligence professional must certify that "it is important."

---

[14] For example, see Roger Hilsman's *Strategic Intelligence and National Decisions* (Glencoe, Il: The Free Press, 1956), 7, 10. A Princeton academic, he explores the notion that "scholars could in some respects take the place of spies," and that academics, especially social scientists, could in the IC "find their real home within the formal structure of government."

[15] Norman Holmes Pearson, Yale graduate and former OSS official, suggested that the CIA recruit its younger personnel from universities and urged that each university have informal talent spotters who would forward names of likely candidates. See Robin W. Winks, *Cloak and Gown: Scholars in the Secret War, 1939-1961* (New York: William Morrow Publishing Company, 1987), 315.

[16] Winks, 14-19, notes that Nathan Hale, a Yale graduate, is of special interest as the first "spy" executed for his work. Other noted Yale personages involved with intelligence activities include: Arnold Wolfers, Sherman Kent, Chester B. Kerr, James Angleton, C. Bradford Wells, Norman Holmes Pearson, Dean Acheson and Richard Bissell.

[17] Edward F. Sayle, "The Historical Underpinning of the U.S. Intelligence Community," *International Journal of Intelligence and Counterintelligence* 1, no. 1 (Spring 1986): 1-17.

Another point of conversation and contention is the responsibility for the ultimate use of information power, whether of technical or human origin. Is the individual who has the information and gives it to the "government" responsible for the ultimate use of that information? Referring to scientific advances in weaponry during World War II: Was a scientist who invented a weapon responsible for the ultimate use of that weapon? If the academic-scientist gave information to the government, did the very nature of government absolve him from guilt if it were to be used in a way not foreseeable by the scientist? Did it matter whether the government was a "dictatorship" or a "democracy"? On the human intelligence side: Were doctors and scientists, conducting scientific experiments on human populations in concentration camps and under the direction of government officials, responsible for the use of that information? What if the information eventually saved lives, albeit those of a Fascist regime? During the Vietnam era, the question was raised in another context: Information concerning populations in Laos, Cambodia, and Vietnam, collected by anthropologists, was subsequently used in support of the war effort. What was the ethical and moral responsibility of the information gatherer? Did they "sell out"? And, if so, what did they sell out to? Is final use of HUMINT the combined responsibility of the collector and disseminator? The ensuing and subsequent debates have been acrimonious, difficult, and divisive.

On the West Coast, and during the Cold War, the strain between academics and the IC contributed to a number of very ugly scenes. Distinctions were made between those academics who were "patriotic, loyal, and anti-communist," and those who challenged authority in any context. Simple questioning became a sign of disloyalty. Universities were increasingly supported by public funding, and administrators were increasingly drawn from a professional management pool rather than from the scholarly community, resulting in a view that universities were simply another form of business enterprise. Administrators were often afraid to allow challenges to government on the part of the faculty out of fear of losing funding. The divisiveness of this period cannot be overemphasized in explaining the nature of the contemporary public university. Administrative penalties for individual scholars included blacklisting, failure to get tenure, lack of research support, and even dismissal from teaching positions. The public presentation of "truth" was simple: teaching loyalty to the country was the real job of the teacher/ academic. Anything contrary was a serious and significant challenge to the future of the nation. And, if the public supported the university both financially and with its "children," it in turn should be able to expect loyalty on the part of its faculty employees. The long-term effects of this controversy were devastating: a certain level of self-censorship on the part of academics, serious mistrust between university administrators and faculty, and reluctance of faculty members to cooperate with intelligence agencies. The communities became unnecessarily, but understandably, polarized.[18]

---

[18] Ellen W. Schrecker, *No Ivory Tower: McCarthyism and the Universities* (New York: Oxford University Press, 1986).

A significant problem for both communities is the strangulation that can occur through bureaucratic-institutional rigidities. The academic community is quite aware that real education *could be* much better but that the *status quo* supports the professoriate; that is, change is always a bit dangerous as it usually means a diminishment of academic independence and an enhancement of administrative power. The IC also would admit to bureaucratic complacency in times of peace. Changes incur costs either in the diminution of capability or loss of institutional "territory." Both the intelligence professional and the academic are, to some extent, prisoners of their own bureaucracies and are habitually resistant to change.

There is an attendant problem: Neither of the communities is monolithic, although that stereotype persists. Most academics do not know the difference between the CIA and DIA nor the nature of their specific mandates from Congress, except perhaps in "wartime," when such differences become more widely known through media coverage. Similarly, intelligence professionals often lump all colleges and universities and hence the professoriate into one big resource group. Intelligence professionals make it their business to know their colleagues in other agencies; academics know who is working on "what," the relative integrity of individuals and institutions, and the unwritten division of labor in the university system. This information is buried in the collective consciousness of each community and remains difficult to exhume—hence the persistence of the monolithic stereotype

Each community has a body of common knowledge which it assumes everyone working within the institutional framework knows and accepts. Because common knowledge is "common," it is not self-conscious and most individuals do not even realize that basic assumptions are seldom challenged. For example: the academic community assumes that books are good and thus libraries should have them. Individuals in the IC often assume that books are inherently historical and that current information and intelligence must be "near-real-time" and continually refreshed. There is a distinct attitude of arrogance when these individuals discuss the currency of information with academics. What is not at issue, of course, is that the intelligence professional has to produce and is charged with an indications and warning responsibility mandating inclusion of current information.

Academics are known for jargon and obfuscation; the IC is known for producing acronyms seemingly at leisure. The tribal languages are difficult to learn without a willing translator. Such facilitators may be hard to find because language serves to define the in-group and the out-group and what can or should be communicated within the organization and to outsiders. To illustrate, the academic community believes that the title "doctor" is best reserved for a medical professional and that the title of "professor" connotes sufficient recognition of achievement. However, the military and intelligence communities rigidly and habitually call academics "doctor," sometimes embarrassing both parties. At the same time, the IC has a specific ranking for directors, analysts, collectors, and techies, and for military and civil service personnel. These are totally obscure for the academic working within the community. They don't know the differences and often do not want to take the time to learn.

Rules of interaction for each group differ significantly. Academics are notoriously fractious and democratic. Anyone can challenge anyone on any idea at any time–and do so. Sometimes it is not very polite or courteous even when the comment begins with: "I understand your premise, *but*, have you considered.....?" Bloodletting is the rule rather than the exception. Members of the IC appear to be more polite although "outsiders" may assume that they derive enjoyment from more discreet disagreement. The various forms of interaction are notable when individuals from the IC quietly participate in sections of the International Studies Association or the Political Science Association, or when academics vociferously contribute to conferences held under the auspices of the IC.

Prejudices and stereotypes held by each group toward the other are often very funny and uncomfortably accurate. The intelligence professional hides in a secure building; the academic retreats to the pie-in-the-sky ivory tower. The intelligence professional is not excessively talkative; the academic cannot be bridled. It is assumed that academics and scholars are in never-never land with theory that cannot be proved or disproved. The intelligence professional is said to live in a land of basic facts without understanding the "big picture." When specifically challenged, both sides recognize that one cannot have facts without theory nor theory without supporting evidence. Yet the stereotypes remain and there is misunderstanding and misinformation on both sides and few venues to correct those that cause problems in communication.

There is further the problem of "group-think" on both sides. Each assumes not infrequently that they have a lock on reality and often simply refuse to be open-minded. This occurred during the Vietnam era when the IC felt itself misunderstood and abused, and the academic community believed that its information and personnel were being used by intelligence agencies in ways of which academe did not approve. The complexity of the story is well-known but the mythology remains extant.[19] Part of the mythology is that intelligence agencies will collect information from academics but not return or share information in a collegial manner. On the other side, the assumption on the part of intelligence professionals is that the academics have a bad attitude and misunderstand or undervalue the IC contribution to national well-being. The academic community believes that it is not afflicted with the IC's tunnel vision and can contribute to lateral thinking that supports enhanced problem-solving capabilities.

THE ACADEMIC'S DECISION

The motivations for an academic to work for the IC are, of course, individualistic and mixed. He or she may simply want a "steady" job that pays well–even if only working over the summer break. There can also be an ego boost when intelligence experts value the information and assessment done by an academic in a particular field. The value attached to being "appreciated" for the information and analysis cannot be overstated as there is very little of that inherent in the academic community. It is also possible that an

---

[19] Note the references to news reports and other material on websites devoted to the use and abuse of intelligence during the Vietnam Era.

academic simply wants a new and important challenge and seeks to contribute to a group effort designed to enhance national security.

A number of problems may emerge if an academic goes to work for the IC, becomes a contractor, or produces information that can be used by that community. He may "go native," that is, become more "intelligence-centric" than the IC needs or desires, all in an attempt to "belong." There is a tendency for self-delusion and thinking that the information contributed is going to "make a difference." Sometimes it does; sometimes it is just part of the package provided for a specific tasking. The academic really has no way of knowing what impact his or her work is having.

There are special areas in which the academic can contribute to the IC. A primary contribution is in the collection of facts and information using sources that the IC is precluded from using. Academics can generally travel more easily than intelligence analysts and can establish human networks across international boundaries that can be very useful especially in times of crisis. Academics generally are trained in the development of analytical frameworks and employ them with a degree of ease and clarity. Many academics contribute a unique ability to critique or evaluate projects based on a wide reading of the literature combined with "on the ground" experience. The good academic is always a perverse thinker–looking to examine the null hypothesis or suggesting alternative explanations. They tend not to accept the "generally accepted explanation." This habit can make them a bit difficult as conversationalists especially if "critique" is translated as "criticism." A good academic scholar will insist on "rigor," as in following the requirement to test basic assumptions, validate criteria used in hypothesis building, monitor the internal validity of hypotheses, and pinpoint the public implications of certain theories. Academic rigor mandates "elegance"; that is, a hypothesis must be important, clear, and predictive. Even in descriptive analysis, an academic insists on looking at a range of possible alternative choices and at the internal coherence of the final product.

There is another caveat: most academics believe that intelligence professionals are better paid and have more job security for doing similar work. This may imply that academics will skew their work in order to get the "big bucks" that the IC is assumed to have sitting in a back room. The serious implication is that there is a potential for academics to give up academic integrity and play to the audience in order to get government contracts. On the other hand, if it is only supplemental income for the professors, the extra income can be very supportive of the academic profession at large. It is worth noting that salaries of academics vary hugely across the spectrum of colleges and universities and in different regions of the country.[20] It must also be noted that if academics are taking up intelligence taskings, they are not generally able at the same time to write for publication in scholarly journals. Participation in conferences is also limited and inter-academic communications suffer as a consequence.

---

[20] Approximately forty percent of all U.S. academic positions are adjunct or part-time. These pay somewhere in the range of $1,500 to $3,000 per class, which roughly translates as $24,000 a year for someone with an advanced, terminal degree.

There are a number of roles that academics can have in the IC: teaching, conducting research, consultation on specific issues, monitoring, evaluating programs, collaborating with other professionals on special projects, and holding conversations on issues of mutual concern. Most of these areas have been exploited to one degree or another. An area that is often overlooked is that of professional development. After all, many professors have spent a great deal of time teaching, testing, and designing learning materials. Not all are good at it–but many have considerable skills that could be tapped. Another specific area is in the teaching of research methodology and specialized writing. Intelligence professionals are sometimes criticized on their ability to effectively and efficiently engage the audience in oral presentations of their ideas and materials. Perhaps specific individuals in the academic community would be helpful in teaching and supporting that skill development.

The ultimate caveat: it is hard to explain to professional colleagues that "I am not a spy." The mystique outlives the reality. It can be overcome with honesty and some degree of good humor.

There are specific benefits to the IC if academics and scholars are employed wisely. One of the often-heard criticisms of the IC is that it has a special susceptibility to "group-think" because analysts seldom have internal challenges. Projects, after all, are group-produced and tend to reduce an individual's unique contribution in favor of the final product. The academic, simply by the nature of the job, challenges the norms, supports individual initiative and creativity, and values novel or unconventional thinking.

SUGGESTIONS FOR MUTUAL SUPPORT
AND MUTUAL BENEFIT

For all of the reasons just noted, it is important that the IC encourage the participation of academics. Academics can make significant contributions in creative thinking, rigor of analysis, and professional presentation of products.

But the choice of which academic to invite as a participant and the venue for participation are not givens. The IC might do well to choose individual academics not for their geographic convenience, near to the Washington or New York areas, but for the written scholarly work produced in their "home environment." Some of the work is apparent at professional conferences such as those of the International Studies Association and the Political Science Association. Some academics, however, do not "conference." They do, however, write and produce articles for journals and books for publication. These individuals can be found by reputation in the community, in reading lists, and in lists of current publications provided by commercial book publishers. Another often-neglected academic source is the database developed by University Microfilms International (UMI) of Ann Arbor, Michigan. Its widely available "Dissertation Abstracts International" indexes over 1.5 million dissertations from the U.S. and some other English-speaking countries.[21]

It matters little whether the academic is familiar or comfortable with intelligence or intelligence agencies: what matters most is honest and clear communication. In the author's first association, I was promised that all materials could and should be "open source" and that I had final say on what information went into the project. Because I was aware of the potential for harm to informants in an ethnic violence situation, this became critical support for my contribution to a specific project.

Think tanks are very peculiar instances of hybridization. What the IC does not often realize is that Rand, Hoover, and Carnegie are assigned specific status by academics. It is assumed that "since they get their money directly from the government," they are somehow tainted. Research is suspect and academic integrity is assumed to have been compromised. Nevertheless, the tanks pay very well and very fine academics contribute substantially to critically needed and specifically targeted research.

Universities are not monolithic. Many will support technical research financed by the U.S. Government, but distance themselves from government "intrusion" in the social sciences. This is understandable but can be challenged if those interested in "public-private" interchange develop or appeal to a board of monitors or research advisors.[22] The IC is not precluded from supporting social-cultural research. There have been any number of works emanating from political science departments on topics relating to democracy and development. Economics departments are enthusiastic contributors to development projects and economic distribution issues. Most universities are giving increased attention to environmental issues including environmental security.[23]

Another touchy but important area is in the potential contribution of information and understanding by visiting foreign students and visiting professors. It is well recognized that using undergraduate students in this sense remains fairly unproductive. There is an ongoing debate about getting information about, tracking, or using graduate students. Certainly the base of internationally focused information available on university cam-

---

[21] The University of Minnesota maintains a database for U.S. Master's theses and Ph.D. dissertations These are abstracted and available through the UMI system. Further information can be found on their respective websites: http://www.lib.umn.edu and http://www.lib.umi.com/dissertations.

[22] Widely used "Institutional Research Boards," for example, could address ethical and other issues even before they arise. For a useful discussion of the role of IRBs, see Bruce L. Berg, *Qualitative Research Methods for the Social Sciences*, 3rd ed. (Boston, MA: Allyn and Bacon, 1998), chapter 3.

[23] Although there is no evidence of specific linkages between the IC and the following examples, these academic authors are often quoted by the IC in support of new models relating intelligence requirements to a broadened definition of security: Jack Snyder, *From Voting to Violence: Democratization and Nationalist Conflict* (New York: W. W. Norton, 2000); Georg Sorensen, *Democracy and Democratization: Processes and Prospects in a Changing World* (Boulder: Westview Press, 1998); James G. March and Johan P. Olsen, Democratic Governance (New York: Free Press, 1995). On environment issues related to security, see *Environmental Conflict*, Paul F. Duiehl and Nils Petter Gleditsch, eds. (Boulder: Westview Press, 2001) and *Ecoviolence: Links among Environment, Population, and Security*, Thomas Homer-Dixon and Jessica Blitt, eds. (Boulder, CO: Rowman & Littlefield Publishers, Inc., 1998).

puses could be more usefully (and publicly) exploited. In the current environment, most universities have been encouraged to check on the legal status of their international students, especially those coming from countries known to support international terrorism. International student offices and university administrators have had mixed reactions. The international students are a source of out-of-state tuition and contribute to the overall diversity of a campus. International student counselors and offices have historically acted as advocates for the guest students. There is some reluctance to take on a "law enforcement" function, however much individuals may support anti-terrorism efforts.

Specific programs have been developed by the CIA and DIA for encouraging academic participation with the IC. These efforts need to be encouraged, regularized, institutionalized, and adequately financed. The Scholars-in-Residence program of the Central Intelligence Agency is well known.[24] The Fulbright Senior Fellowship program, funded through the Department of State, is invaluable. Most informal or formal interaction takes place through individual consulting, sponsorship and organization of topical conferences, funding of individuals for specific research of mutual interest and concern, funding and support for research centers, and informal conversations at any one of the periodic, internationally focused academic conferences. This interaction can be highly productive because both parties tend to focus on international issues of mutual concern, and bring special expertise to bear for creative and constructive problem solving.

CONCLUSION

Academics and intelligence professionals are concerned with much the same set of problems. The approaches to problem solving may differ but certainly the practices inherent in American democratic tradition have constructed the intellectual environment so as to provide common definitions of contemporary threats and challenges. Both communities agree that liberty, democracy, freedom, equality, law, and property are defensible American values. Cooperation between the IC and academics, and specific contributions that academics can make to the production of good intelligence, can and must be further supported. It would be foolish to waste available skills and talent. There is too much at stake.

BIBLIOGRAPHY

Berg, Bruce L. *Qualitative Research Methods for the Social Sciences*, 3rd ed. Boston, MA: Allyn and Bacon, 1998.

Duiehl, Paul F. and Nils Petter Gleditsch, eds. *Environmental Conflict*. Boulder, CO: Westview Press, 2001.

---

[24] See Gates, 1986. A more recent status report on ties between CIA and professional academics is in Lloyd D. Salvetti, Director, Center for the Study of Intelligence, "Teaching Intelligence: Working Together to Build a Discipline," in *Teaching Intelligence at Colleges and Universities*, Proceedings of the 18 June 1999 JMIC Conference (Washington, DC: JMIC, 1999), 12-24.

Gates, Robert M. "CIA and the University," *Studies in Intelligence* 30, no. 2 (Summer 1986): 27-36.

Hilsman, Roger. *Strategic Intelligence and National Decisions*. Glencoe, IL: The Free Press, 1956.

Holt, Pat M. *Secret Intelligence and Public Policy: A Dilemma of Democracy*. Washington, DC: CQ Press, 1995.

Homer-Dixon, Thomas and Jessica Blitt, eds. *Ecoviolence: Links among Environment, Population and Security*. Boulder, CO: Rowman and Littlefield Publishers, 1998.

March, James G. and Johan P. Olsen. *Democratic Governance*. New York: Free Press, 1995.

Salvetti, Lloyd D. "Teaching Intelligence: Working Together to Build a Discipline." In *Teaching Intelligence at Colleges and Universities*, Proceedings of the 18 June 1999 JMIC Conference. Washington, DC: JMIC, 1999.

Sayle, Edward F. "The Historical Underpinnings of the U.S. Intelligence Community." *International Journal of Intelligence and Counterintelligence* 1, no. 1(Spring 1986): 1-17.

Schrecker, Ellen W. *No Ivory Tower: McCarthyism and the Universities*. New York: Oxford University Press, 1986.

Snyder, Jack. *From Voting to Violence: Democratization and Nationalist Conflict*. New York: W.W. Norton, 2000.

Sorensen, Georg. *Democracy and Democratization: Processes and Prospects in a Changing World*. Boulder, CO: Westview Press, 1998.

Turner, Stansfield. *Secrecy and Democracy: The CIA in Transition*. Boston, MA: Houghton Mifflin Company, 1985.

Winks, Robin W. *Cloak and Gown: Scholars in the Secret War*, 1939-1961. New York: William Morrow Publishing Company, 1987.

ABOUT THE AUTHOR

Dr. John Turner is the senior Middle East and North Africa analyst at the U.S. European Command's Joint Analysis Center, where he is responsible for strategic estimates. His past assignments concerned with the Middle East and Africa region include estimative, counterintelligence, and current intelligence analytical postings in the U.S. and Europe. He has traveled widely in the Middle East and Africa. Dr. Turner earned degrees in Near Eastern Languages and Literatures from the University of Michigan and Yale University.

VIA THE INTERNET:
NEWS AND INFORMATION FOR THE ANALYST
FROM NORTH AFRICAN ELECTRONIC MEDIA

John Turner

The remarkable growth of electronic media over the past decade in Francophone North Africa provides specialists in the region with a wealth of news and other information. This survey and analysis of the French-language media of Algeria, Morocco, and Tunisia examines how these media go about providing information on North African politics, economics, and culture in a way that does take account of expatriates, who make up an important sector of the politically active population. For "outsiders" who specialize in the interpretation of the region, news media offer a "grass-roots"-based prism through which future developments may be anticipated.[1] Observable trends in the North Africa media, when carefully documented and placed in context, validate the contention of various authors, from Robert Steele and Gregory Treverton to Arthur Hulnick, who have addressed the promises and perils of devoting a greater share of intelligence resources to the exploitation open-source information. They have found much more promise than peril.[2]

REGIONAL MEDIA CULTURE

The political context in which North African media have evolved over the past three decades is chiefly one of centralized governments tending toward authoritarianism, be it oligarchical in the case of Algeria, monarchical in the case of Morocco, or presidential in the case of Tunisia. The political institutions of each country developed separately in the post-colonial period and in each country a different media culture exists that has until now clearly defined the role of the broadcast and print media. However, through the 1990s, as Internet access and use spread to the region, the public in each country, as well as the expatriate North African communities in Europe and elsewhere are proving to be a major

---

[1] An early and prescient example of this approach to "futurology" is in John Naisbitt's *Megatrends* (New York: Warner Books, 1982). Naisbitt's approach to trendspotting was to scan thousands of local newspapers in the U.S. and to extrapolate trends unobtrusively from those "grass roots" sources. This approach is explained in pages 8-9 of the book.

[2] For example, see Steele's *On Intelligence: Spies and Secrecy in an Open World* (Fairfax, VA: AFCEA International Press, 2002); Treverton's *Reshaping National Intelligence for an Age of Information* (Cambridge, UK: Cambridge University Press, 2001), chapter Four; Hulnick, "The Downside of Open Source Intelligence," *International Journal of Intelligence and CounterIntelligence* 15, no. 4 (Winter 2002-2003): 565-579.

new political factor.[3] This development results from the web's provision of news, including both analysis and opinion, as well as useful business information. Governments now experience strong competition from non-state run media due in large part to the use by the latter of the Internet.[4]

The political and business elites in Algeria, Morocco, and Tunisia have spearheaded the public demand for information to support their routine decisionmaking. Exposed increasingly over the past four decades to European and other media, North Africans desire that their domestic media mirror standards set elsewhere in the region and the world. It is in the electronic versions of the region's print media that this expectation has been most fully realized. Since the late 1990s a host of daily and weekly periodicals have developed electronic news sites, most backed by their parent print news organizations. Although the discussion here focuses on the French-language dimensions of this phenomenon, the reader should be aware that in each country a rapidly growing Arabic electronic media culture exists as well.

SURVEY OF NORTH AFRICAN ELECTRONIC NEWS MEDIA

Algeria

Algeria's electronic media culture is dominated by Internet versions of the country's French and Arabic-language newspapers. For the former, there are a dozen Algiers-based dailies and one Oran-based daily that cater to audiences in Algeria and Europe (see table below). Electronic versions of Algerian newspapers began in the early 1990s to provide the Algerian community abroad, especially in France, with news.[5] As of late 2002 thirteen dailies[6] are available on the Internet, all regularly maintained and updated daily. Algerian dailies are increasingly user-friendly and most have undergone facelifts as they make a bid for an increasingly sophisticated audience at home and abroad. Generally these

---

[3] Naturally, this development is recognized by those predisposed to shape public opinion. On the information-media contest between religious and secular forces, see Dale F. Eickelman, "The Coming Transformation in the Muslim World," *Current History* 99, no. 633 (January 2000): 16-20. For further background, see Eickelman's book, *New Media in the Muslim World: The Emerging Public Sphere* (Bloomington, IN: Indiana University Press, 1999).

[4] For discussions of the pre-Internet media in North Africa during the Cold War era, see especially the U.S. Army publications *Algeria: A Country Study*, fourth edition, 1985, 268-271; *Morocco: A Country Study*, fifth edition, 1985, 277-280; and *Tunisia: A Country Study*, third edition, 1986, 249-252. For coverage of post-Internet media developments, see *http://www.hrw.org/advocacy/internet/mena/index.htm*.

[5] See Elias Hanna Elias, *La Presse arabe* (Paris: Maisonneuve & Larose, 1993), 94. The government press monopoly was only ended in 1988. A snapshot of the evolving press culture in Algeria in the early 1990s is given in the fifth edition of *Algeria: A Country Study*, 1994, 218-220.

[6] One of them, *L'Expression*, was dormant for most the month of November 2002, reappearing at the end of the month after a remake (*www.lexpressiondz.com*). Such episodes are common with other electronic dailies in Algeria, which can unexpectedly be down for long periods of time while their web sites are redesigned.

changes have seen progressive upgrades in graphics quality, reliability of links, and web page format. In late 2002 alone, two dailies, *Liberte* and *Le Soir d'Algerie,* have both undergone major changes in the "look and feel" of their web sites.

Name	Internet address	Remarks
L'Actualitie	www.lactualite-dz.com	Independent; pdf format only
L'Authentique	www.authentique-dz.com	Independent
L'Expression	www.lexpressiondz.com	Independent; connections with government
Horizons	www.horizons-dz.com	Independent
Le Jeune Independant	www.jeune-independant.com	Independent
Liberte	www.liberte-algerie.com	Independent
Le Matin	www.lematin-dz.com	Connections with Interior Ministry
Al-Moudjahid	www.elmoudjahid-dz-com	Newspaper of the FLN, the ex-state party
La Nouvelle Republique	www.lanouvellerepublique.com	Independent
Le Quotidien d'Oran	www.quotidien-oran.com	Independent; main French-language daily in Western Algeria; published in Oran.
Le Soir d'Algerie	www.lesoiralgerie.com	Independent; principal independent evening French daily
La Tribune	www.latribune-online.com	Independent
El Watan	www.elwatan.com	National daily of record; connections to Army

Algerian French-Language Daily Newspapers on the Internet

In contrast to the wealth of dailies represented in the electronic media, there is a dearth of Algerian weeklies available on the Internet. Some of the daily web sites have "week-end"-oriented articles appearing in their Thursday or Saturday editions (Algerian papers and their electronic counterparts are not issued on Friday). However, only three of them at the time of writing had multimedia "magazine" supplements.[7]

Algeria's government news site is the Algerian Press Service (APS),[8] which has web pages in Arabic, French, English, and Spanish. APS has news offices throughout Algeria and updates its web page of news items daily. Many of the news dailies discussed below use APS reports. However, most have their own network of reporters throughout Algeria and rely upon APS and international wire services for foreign news.

Daily press summaries are provided on two independent web sites. The first is offered by Agence Algerienne d'Information (AAI),[9] which has a detailed daily press review covering the headlines of the nation's French and Arabic language newspapers. A briefer ver-

---

[7] These were the *Jeune Independant* ("JI Multimedia"), *Le Matin* (*MultiM@tin*), and *La Tribune* ("*La Tribune Multimedia*"). In addition, *Le Matin* had a topical section updated every several weeks.

[8] *www.aps.dz.*

[9] *www.aai-online.com/revu.*

sion of the country's daily press offering is found on the website of the "Algeria Guide."[10] *El Watan*[11] is one of the oldest of the electronic dailies appearing on the web, and caters to a French-speaking audience at home and abroad. El Watan is widely cited as a news daily of record.

In addition to the French-language dailies noted in the table, one cannot ignore Algeria's leading Arabic language daily, *El Khabar*.[12] Starting in 2001, daily editions of this paper in Arabic have been supplemented by English and French headlines pages.[13] Each consists of a brief summary of the daily print and electronic edition's major stories. Although the English and French sites are similar, the choice of items for summarization from the Arabic original is not all-inclusive. Nevertheless, these pages are important for non-Arabic readers as an insight into the reporting focus of Algeria's largest daily.

Morocco

In contrast to Algeria's thriving daily Internet news culture, Moroccan electronic news media represent a combination of daily and weekly web sites. The daily print news providers and their electronic web sites (see table below) are dominated by four major papers. However, the news culture of Morocco is also marked by a strong showing of news weeklies, many of which are relatively new since the end of the 1990s and the accession of the present monarch, King Mohamed VI, to the throne.

Name	Internet address	Remarks
Al-Bayane	*www.casanet.net.ma/albayane/*	Casablanca; French-language daily of the PPS
Liberation	*www.liberation.press.ma*	Casablanca; French-language daily of the USFP
Le Matin du Sahara et du Maghreb	*www.lematin.ma*	Casablanca; government/royalist news daily
L'Opinion	*www.lopinion.ma*	Casablanca; French-language daily of the Istiqlal
L'Economiste	*www.leconomiste.com*	Casablanca; independent daily specializing in business and commercial news
Le Quotidien du Maroc	*www.casanet.net.ma/quotidien*	Casablanca; Independent daily

Moroccan French-Language Daily Newspapers on the Internet

Moroccan dailies have been appearing in electronic form since 1998, when the semi-official *Le Matin du Maghreb et du Sahara* began Internet publication. *Le Matin* was later followed by the newspapers of three of the political parties of the center-left Koutla coalition in the parliament. These papers still form the backbone of the electronic daily publi-

---

[10] *www.algerie-guide.com/actualitie.*

[11] *El Watan: Le Quotidien Independant, http://www.elwatan.com.*

[12] *www.elkhabar.com.* Links to the French and English headline pages are found on the main page of the daily edition.

[13] *www.elkhabar.com/html/pageAnglais.html* and *www.elkhabar.com/html/pageFrancais.html*

cation, joined only by the independent *L'Economiste* and *Le Quotidien du Maroc*. Morocco's news dailies are still largely the domain of its political parties.[14]

Morocco's national news agency is the *Maghreb Arabe Presse* (MAP),[15] which has web sites in English, French, Arabic, and Spanish. MAP, as well as international wire services, provides domestic news dailies with foreign news and some domestic news items. MAP hosts a French web site that provides a daily press review of nineteen French and Arabic dailies.[16]

Le Matin du Maghreb et du Sahara has the largest print circulation and its web version also dominated the electronic media after its 1998 launch. However, the first web site was extensively overhauled in September 2001, changing from one primarily mirroring the print edition to one with distinctive content that was also distinguished with a distinct name—*Le Matin.ma*[17]—to emphasize its web status.

Tunisia

Tunisia's electronic press remains restricted compared to that in Algeria and Morocco, with the country's Internet activity subject to close government scrutiny. The paucity of news dailies (see table below) and the availability of foreign print media at the present time combine with government controls to produce an electronic media culture that focuses heavily on business and commerce, as well as non-controversial domestic and foreign news items.

Name	Internet address	Remarks
La Presse du Tunisie	www.tunisie.com/LaPresse/index.html	Principal French-language daily; government connections
Le Renoveau	www.tunisieinfo.com/LeRenoveau/	French-language daily of the RCD, the dominant political party in Tunisia.
Le Temps	www.tunisie.com/Assabah/Alternate: www.lapress.tn	French daily published by Dar es-Sebah, Tunis

Tunisian French-Language Daily Newspapers on the Internet

Tunisia's news dailies are heavily controlled by the government, with even the country's largest non-government press house, Dar es-Sebah, having to keep within unofficial but very real constraints.[18]

---

[14] Elias, 109.

[15] *www.map.co.ma.*

[16] *www.map.co.ma/mapfr/fr.*

[17] *www.lematin.ma.*

[18] See Elias, 108-109, for the major Tunisian press enterprises, of which *Dar es-Sebah* is one.

MEDIA ISSUES: OBJECTIVITY AND ACCURACY

The political heritage of North Africa and its impact on the region's media culture together raise the inevitable questions of editorial freedom, objectivity and accuracy. The ideal standard for North African publications, as in other countries, is one of adherence to strict standards of reporting and analyzing events in a climate of universal press freedom. However, "red lines" exist in editorial freedom, objectivity, and accuracy that are perilous to cross. North African media have suffered negative sanctions imposed by government officials as the result of reporting that has broken taboos.[19]

Objectivity is a concern for analysts and researchers in a media culture where most papers, not only those owned by manifestly political groups, but also the independent press, are controlled by interests that have a marked political agenda. Nevertheless, in both Algeria and Morocco a system of checks and balances exists, with daily and weekly print media and their electronic counterparts in vigorous competition for the domestic and foreign market. These publications maintain high standards of journalism, and are normally quite open about their particular biases or journalistic objectives. Such competition and declared interests ensure a degree of confidence in political and economic analysis that allows a high degree of confidence among business and government consumers who seek information for decisionmaking. Tunisia, with its dearth of news dailies and strong government influence in the media, remains problematic for the area specialist seeking in-depth analysis of some events, although most economic and business reporting remains of high quality and supports its citizens' decisionmaking effectively.[20]

Accuracy has historically been less of a concern. A flourishing media culture and rivalry among news dailies and weeklies in Algeria and Morocco ensures a degree of competition that normally means news items are reliable; that is, consistently reported in different publications with a sufficient degree of detail and verification of factual data to make them satisfactory records of events. In such an information-rich climate, attempts by government or private parties to plant stories would be subject to immediate scrutiny and detection by the press. The latter frequently analyzes government reporting on an issue and takes it to task for various shortcomings, thereby ensuring, through the resulting reliability, that validity or accuracy is also addressed.

NORTH AFRICAN MEDIA AS A SOURCE OF INFORMATION

The electronic media in Algeria, Morocco, and Tunisia remain tied to their print media roots. This is an economic necessity, as too few in these countries lack the disposable income to rely on the Internet as their main source of information. Printed newspapers,

---

[19] Recent problems encountered by journalists include cutoff of advertising support in Tunisia (*El Maoukif*, 21 December 2001), as well as outright government seizure of publications in Morocco (*Al Mostaqil*, 1 May 2002).

[20] For the Arab world as a whole, these observations are supported by Dale F. Eickerman, "The Arab 'Street' and the Middle East's Democracy Deficit," *Naval War College Review* 55, no. 4 (Autumn 2002): 39-48.

either daily or weekly, are relatively cheap and widely available, and within the means of most of the region's population. So long as the region's economic problems continue, there will be limits on disposable income that impact the ability of the electronic media to be of practical use to its intended audience.

Databases, and their extent and degree of searchability, remain issues for the researcher. In terms of media-based interpretation of North African countries, there is little consistency in whether or not an electronic daily or weekly has links to past editions, and how easily they can be accessed and searched. The majority of electronic news media still offer no search capability, forcing readers to access past editions one by one in the hope of finding specific news items. Media storage capabilities often limit web sites from offering more than a few months' worth of past issues. Certain publications, such as those of the Moroccan *L'Economiste, La Vie Economique*, and *Maroc Hebdo*, are prominent exceptions. But with most other electronic publications from the region, the researcher's quest is often frustrated by lack of archival depth and broken links. Remedies to the current deficiencies will be slow in coming and dependent on additional data storage availability and improved website management.

Reporting of events, as noted above, is as objective and accurate as that found anywhere in the world. The electronic media in Algeria and Morocco are often the single best source of news for outside researchers who try to interpret the climate of opinion and incipient trends that exist in the interior of these large and increasingly complex countries. Local news is a growth industry in Morocco, but has yet to become well-established in Algeria or Tunisia. However, the steady growth of electronic media and the institutionalization of its culture as a normal supplement to the print world promises that local newspapers will soon be much more available in electronic form via the Internet. Such sites, however, are as likely to be in Arabic as in French, depending upon the local population and the degree to which the outlet has an expatriate readership.

Electronic news media are slowly but certainly being augmented by independent Internet sites. Such sites are still relatively few due to their lacking a solid print media base to finance electronic editions. However, the provisional success of *CasaNet* in Morocco[21] and *Cirta* in Algeria[22] probably indicate a proliferation of these sources.

---

[21] *www.casanet.net.ma* is the web site address of *Menara: La Portail du Maroc*, hosted by Morocco's largest telecommunications company, Maroc Telecom. Menara previously hosted the Moroccan electronic dailies *Liberation* and *al-Bayane*, but both now have their own independent sites.

[22] *www.cirtaonline.com/news/* has a constantly updated listing of world, national, and local news. Despite its name (Cirta is the old Roman name for the eastern Algerian city of Constantine), the site is national in scope, leaving local news to the Arabic-language daily *an-Nasr* (*www.an-nasr.com*).

It remains uncertain whether electronic news dailies or weeklies will come to dominate the Internet news market in North Africa. Much depends on the fortunes of their parent print media companies, trends in the news-reading public's interests, and the rate of growth of the local economies in North Africa and the amount of disposable income available to the general population to sustain further growth of the electronic media. Until personal computers and affordable Internet access is commonly available, most North Africans will still rely on the print and broadcast media as their primary forms of news information. In this situation, access by the public to the Internet will remain largely confined to the "Internet Cafes" that are burgeoning throughout the region. Such a situation will sustain only modest electronic media growth.

Under these circumstances, it is likely that one of the key factors in the growth of North African electronic media is likely to be the expatriate community in Europe.[23] The latter enjoy sufficient disposable income and have the motivation to make use of the Internet to follow events in their countries of origin, including at the local or community level. The increased interest by European business and government professionals in North African affairs also provides a potential growth market for electronic media. These professionals often seek and indeed require more information beyond the apparent wealth of data currently available. Catering to such audiences—the expatriate and foreign business/government community—will tend to ensure that in the electronic media world French (and possibly English) news availability will dominate, despite likely future gains by Arabic in the print media world in North Africa itself.

OUTLOOK: INCREASED COVERAGE, GREATER DEPTH

In general, North African, electronic French-language news media still follow the lead of their print counterparts. This is due to the limited access of the population to computers and the Internet, and the continued reliance of the public on broadcast and print media. Further, most media advertisers remain wary of investment in Internet sites, a factor that limits them to being sponsored by established media interests, such as the print media. Nevertheless, the growing number of home computers and Internet connections is bringing the first steps of transformation.

For observers of North African affairs, trends in the French-language electronic news media are reassuring for the near future. Area specialists and other interested professionals will have a steadily growing body of information from which they can draw

---

[23]The North African community in Western Europe numbers approximately two million. For details on numbers and other particulars, see Sarah Colinson, *Shore to Shore: The Politics of Migration in Euro-Maghreb Relations* (London: Royal Institute for International Affairs/Middle East Programme, 1996), especially the table on page 102; and *Migration aus Nordafrika: Ursachen und Problem*, ed. Michaela Koller (Martinsried, Germany: Ars Una, 2000), especially 8ff. and 60ff.

for a reasonably authentic representation of social trends. If political, economic, and social information remains readily available without the geographic limitations associated with print media distribution, the confidence level in information associated with this region among government and business interests worldwide will continue to improve. The ability of North African intelligence specialists to take advantage of multiple rather than single-source information to provide analysis to decisionmakers will, however, increasingly have to take account of Arabic-language media as well as independent Internet news sites in order to ensure a more complete picture of events.

ABOUT THE AUTHOR

Early in his career, as operations officer on the WWII Fletcher-Class destroyer USS *Benham* (DD796), **CAPT George Satterthwaite** became intrigued by the international aspects of being a U.S. Navy officer. The Benham was about to be transferred to Peru under the Military Assistance Program, and he was to accompany a Peruvian crew to Norfolk for underway training, and then go on to Callao where the re-christened *Villar* was to be the flagship of the Peruvian Navy. But he was transferred instead to the Naval Academy to teach calculus. After a tour on a diesel submarine, he left active service, and joined the inactive reserves. Twenty-two years later, in 1986, he discovered that the Navy was looking for individuals to serve attaché duty in hard-to-fill jobs in the Third World. Peru was on the list, and he soon began training and education to become Navy DATT/ALUSNA (Defense Attaché/American Legation U.S. Naval Attaché) in Lima. As he was about to enter Spanish language training, his assignment to Latin America was cancelled, and he was reassigned to be ALUSNA New Delhi where he served for four years from 1988 to 1992.

Having enjoyed his tour in India immensely, CAPT Satterthwaite asked to be reassigned to another Defense Attaché Office (DAO), and was sent to Jakarta for three years (1993 to 1996). During his last year in Jakarta he remarked to his Navy personnel detailer that he had enjoyed the 10 years of active duty time despite the fact that he did not get to go to Peru. The detailer exclaimed that he was having a very tough time filling the DATT/ALUSNA job in Lima, and asked CAPT Satterthwaite to apply once more. At age 60 CAPT Satterthwaite and his wife entered language training for the third time and, after a few months at the Defense Language Institute, went to Lima for a two-year assignment. UNITAS, the large Western Hemisphere, Navy-to-Navy exercise, was inaugurated in the year CAPT Satterthwaite was originally supposed to go to Peru (1960). In 1998 and 1999 he oversaw the planning and implementation of the 38th and 39th cruises. He ended his career as a Naval Attaché in a ceremony officiated by the Chief of Staff of the Peruvian Navy, who had been on the Villar (ex-Benham) as a junior officer. Also in attendance at that ceremony was CAPT Satterthwaite's relief on the Benham, VADM (Ret) Daniel Mariscal. Coincidentally, VADM Mariscal was a 1954 graduate of the U.S. Naval Academy, and CAPT Satterthwaite's father had been his sponsor.

Between active duty assignments, CAPT Satterthwaite had a varied and diverse career. In 1979, he earned a Ph.D. in Public Administration and later taught at The American University, the Naval War College and the Monterey Institute of International Studies. He was also an operations research analyst at the Johns Hopkins University Applied Physics Laboratory, and has served as a consultant to federal, state, local and tribal governments. He now teaches occasionally at the Defense Resource Management Institute, volunteers his time teaching math in a local high school, and is a member of the Monterey County, California, Civil Grand Jury.

VISIT TO MAZAGON DOCKYARD, BOMBAY

F.G. (George) Satterthwaite, CAPT, USNR (Ret.)

Often there are many interesting places an attaché wants to see in the host country, but sometimes the host government is not willing to grant permission for the visit. Sometimes it is a matter of equity. Sometimes permission is not granted because the host has a memorandum of understanding with another country to forbid others to see mutual development projects. At other times the host just considers the places to be visited too sensitive to allow foreigners to see what they are up to.[1] At still other times denial of permission to visit is due to a "we've never done that before, so why let someone do it now" syndrome. The story related here is an example of that kind of response.

During my tour as DATT in Lima, I struck up a friendship with the Commander of the Peruvian Submarine Force. He had just returned from Germany where he had been the Defense and Naval Attaché. He understood the value of promoting good will with others by permitting foreign attachés to observe military operations of a training nature. He knew his attaché in Washington had been taken aboard U.S. nuclear submarines, and had visited the National Training Center at Fort Irwin. He wanted to reciprocate and offered me an eight-hour training ride on one of the Peruvian submarines. He made this offer on the spur of the moment without checking with his Director of Naval Intelligence. He probably thought, as I did, that because Peru has U.S. submarines, allowing a U.S. Naval Attaché on a U.S.-produced submarine would not be a violation of their security rules. The Admiral's offer was made in the weeks just before tensions between Peru and Ecuador heated up, during the summer of 1998. When I called to find out when the trip was scheduled, the Admiral's aide said that all the subs were on alert and he didn't know when the next training ride would take place. This was a totally expected and reasonable response given the operational situation.

---

[1] Defense Attaché officers are bound by the "Vienna Convention on Diplomatic Relations and Optional Protocols[,] Done at Vienna [Austria] on 18 April 1961, U.N.T.S. Nos. 7310-7312, vol. 500, 95-239 (see copy at URL: *http://www.fletcher.tufts.edu/multi/texts/BH408.txt*). These guidelines allow for accredited embassy officials, including military attachés, to engage in "ascertaining by all lawful means conditions and developments in the receiving State, and reporting thereon to the Government of the sending State (Article 3), and provide for freedom of movement except in specifically denied areas (Article 26). For a thorough overview of the "Defense Attaché System," see the Defense Intelligence Agency's *Communique* 12, no. 5 (September/October 2000).

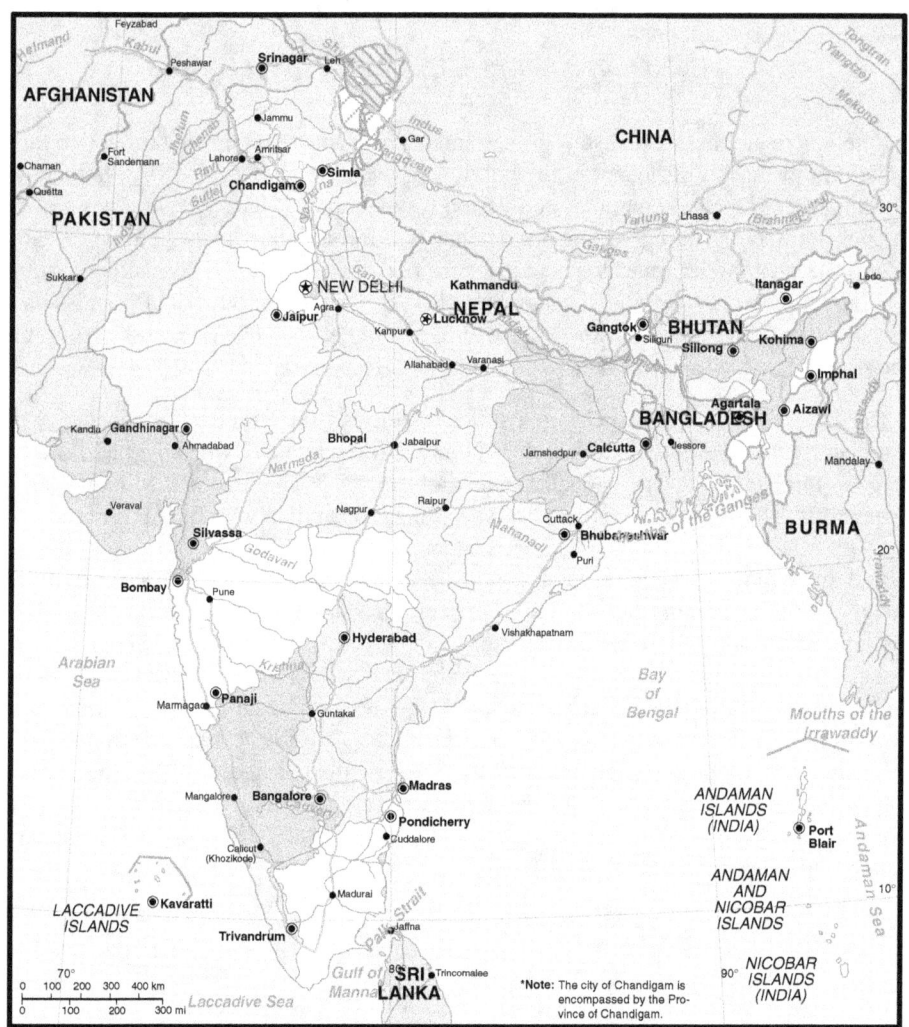

*Note: The city of Chandigam is encompassed by the Province of Chandigam.

As soon as the hostilities were brought to a peaceful conclusion on 26 November 1998, I tried to find another date for the promised submarine ride. The Admiral's aide told me they were trying to find a time and he would get back to me soon. He kept putting me off. As my tour wound down and my relief came to Lima for an orientation to the environment and to the job, I planned a reception and invited the Submarine Commander, among others whom my relief would need to know after he relieved me. The Admiral told me at that time that the visit was a "go," and that it would happen in the final week of my tour. During the last week of my tour the Foreign Liaison Officer took me out to lunch and he told me that the Director of Naval Intelligence (DNI) had countermanded the submarine Admiral's kind offer to let me ride on a Peruvian submarine. The reason given was it would be counter to the national security interests of Peru. The Admiral was totally embarrassed as was the Foreign Liaison Officer, and the Peruvian Navy did not get to show the flag to a friend. The idea of reciprocity did not seem to enter the DNI's mind. Building a good service-to-service relationship moves ahead when friendly attachés are allowed to see how the host services train and operate.

How does an attaché allay either national security concerns or wrong thinking on the part of host-country foreign intelligence officials? In my experience, it is useful to take advantage of visits by "high rollers" to the country. A high roller is a flag or equivalent-level civilian who comes either invited by the host or self-invited by the U.S. Government. Generally, combatant command commanders self-invite themselves once every year or so to the countries in their Area of Responsibility. Fleet commanders of forward-deployed ships also like to visit countries in their operations area that have ports or navies. Self-invited visits generally result in gaining access to military units, which the attaché may have had difficulty visiting on his own. Superior to the self-invited visit is the visit sponsored by the host. Counterpart visits by chiefs of service fall under this heading. Here the host country is usually trying to put a best foot forward to impress the visitor with the capabilities of the host military and may be more amenable to showing off new capabilities and units.

Because the attaché is in a position to recommend an itinerary in both the invited and self-invited visits to the invitee as well as the host, he or she can influence the visit by recommending interesting places for that visitor to see. The only times I was able to see India's Mazagon Dockyard was when the U.S. Chief of Naval Operations (CNO) visited on two different occasions (host-invited visits), and when the staff of the Senate Select Committee on Intelligence (on a self-invited visit) traveled to India to investigate high-tech developments there. The Government of India accepted both of the CNO visits to the dockyard to see submarine developments as natural requests, because both CNOs were submarine officers (ADM Trost and ADM Kelso). I accompanied both CNOs on these visits and had a firsthand look at the Indian Navy's first submarine construction project. There were no repercussions in making these two visits. In fact, the Indian Navy asked me afterward what the CNO thought about their capability to build submarines. They were looking for acceptance as a modern and capable navy from the chief of the world's most modern navy. It was the self-invited visit by the Senate Select Committee on Intelligence staff to Mazagon Dockyard that gave me heartburn.

Several months before the Gulf War it was announced during the embassy's country team meeting that three members of the staff of the Senate Select Committee on Intelligence planned to visit India to see firsthand evidence of India's shipbuilding, aircraft building, atomic research, and space research programs. The staff members were senior U.S. Government employees, at least one of whom was a senior executive civil service or, in military terms, a flag-level visitor. Typically in U.S. embassies around the world, visits by congressional members or staff are under the auspices of the Political Section. This was the case for the Senate Select Committee Staff visit. A control officer from the Political Section was assigned the task of coordinating the visit. His job was to find out what the Staff wanted to accomplish in India, and then present a proposed program agenda to the Foreign Ministry expressing the desires of the self-invitees. After informal acceptance of the proposal, the control officer drafted a diplomatic note and passed it around the embassy for coordination. It was at this point that I learned the visitors would be traveling to Bombay to see the Mazagon Dockyard and Bhaba Atomic Research Laboratory. From Bombay they would travel to the South India version of Silicon Valley at Bangalore, and visit Hindustan Aeronautics Ltd, and the Indian Space Research Organization (ISRO).

Author talks with an Indian Navy captain on board a third-party vessel.
This and other photos courtesy of the author.

I called on the control officer and found he was not overly excited about his responsibilities. He didn't want to travel with the visitors and complained of having too many other responsibilities. Also, the Department of State budget was very tight that year, and the Political Counselor didn't know where the money for travel was going to come from. I immediately interpreted the control officer's protests as a plea to pass the baton of handling this group to someone else. I told him I would be more than happy to take the burden from him. My boss and his agreed to the switch, and I drafted a change to the diplomatic note indicating I would be the new control officer. I did not realize at that time that to propose something to the Indian Foreign Ministry that was a little different from their expectations would make them attribute suspicious intentions to me. I'm sure the old India hands in the embassy, like the Deputy Chief of Mission, had experience with the mindset of Indian bureaucrats, but they did not advise me about the potential for Indian xenophobia to be translated into casting a pall over my bona fides.

I went about coordinating the visit by contacting the visitors and making arrangements for their travel and transportation within India. They arrived in country a week later and we consolidated the plans for the trip to Bombay and Bangalore. Early on a Monday morning we departed from Indira Ghandi International Airport on an Indian Airlines flight to Bombay. Until this point everything was going as planned. Upon arrival in Bombay we hired a cab and took the 25-kilometer ride to the Taj Intercontinental Hotel, past the two million people in the city's slums and over the series of interconnected islands that make up Greater Bombay. We checked into the very posh Taj Intercontinental Hotel, which overlooks the Gateway to India, a memorial to the visit of King George V completed early in the 20th century. I asked for my usual room on the 14th floor, because besides overlooking the *Gateway of India*, it has a panoramic view of Bombay harbor. Fortunately, the room was vacant, and it was assigned to me. After checking in and unloading my suitcase, I peered out the window to see what there was to see in the harbor.

I always looked forward to trips to Bombay because my favorite restaurant there was the Nanking. It was a Chinese restaurant specializing in seafood dishes at very reasonable prices. It was on the ground floor in the same building as the Royal Bombay Yacht Club, and it was only a short walk from the hotel. Their crab with lobster sauce was especially delicious.

The Gateway to India and naval facilities in Bombay.

Author and son visiting with a Hindu holyman at a curio shop in Bombay.

The service in the Nanking was superb. My meal of crab with lobster sauce lived up to expectations, and after a cup of green tea I left the restaurant.

Later that day we visited the Bhaba Atomic Research Center located about mid-way between the hotel and Mazagon Dockyard. We were given the regular visiting-fireman type of tour. We did not observe any advanced research projects, but we did see a reactor used for medical isotope development and were given a watered-down briefing covering the entire research program. Even though we weren't shown the whole nine yards, so to speak, the staffers were impressed at the level of technical sophistication and knowledge of the researchers at the lab. Because their mission was to gauge overall technical competence and not specific programs, the visit to the Bhaba Atomic Research Center was successful.

The next morning we were escorted to the Dockyard, and got a windshield tour of the production facilities by company car. We also saw the work in progress on Soviet-designed destroyers and fast patrol boats. Modular construction of the destroyer was very impressive, and we were also given a status report on the production schedule. Submarine construction was left off the tour, but the chief executive officer of all the Indian-owned shipyards briefed us. He told us of the highlights and shortcomings of the entire Indian shipbuilding industry (military and commercial). All in all, the entire visit to Bombay was more than I had hoped for. One more night in teeming Bombay and we would be off to Bangalore in the morning.

We took the morning Indian Airlines flight to Bangalore, aboard an Airbus 320, of the same type that had crashed a year or so earlier due to a faulty fly-by-wire system. We were fortunate this time. The plane was on time and the flight uneventful.

Bangalore is a much less hectic city than Bombay. It also is populated with a large middle class of educated professionals. Unlike Bombay with some very rich and millions of poverty-stricken citizens, Bangalore is more homogeneous in terms of the standard of living. It is also the hub of technical innovation in India. Many computer firms, to include Hindustan Aeronautics Ltd. and the Indian Space Research Organization (ISRO) are the main centers of technology there. Because of the high density of well-educated and sophisticated people in Bangalore, one finds more Western style retail business establishments there as well. Many of the professional class were educated in the UK or the U.S. and have acquired tastes for Western food and clothing. The *sari* is still commonly worn; hence adoption of Western clothing style is limited to the male population. Bangalore is located in Karnataka State in South India and the local language is Kanada. Kanada, like other South Indian languages, is very different in sound, vocabulary and grammar from the interrelated languages of the North (Hindi, Punjabi, Marathi, Bengali, Bihari, and the like). Hindi speakers cannot understand Kanada speakers and vice versa, so communication between them is usually in English.

We checked into the Taj West End hotel, a member of the same chain as the Taj Intercontinental in Bombay and Taj Village in Goa. It is a one-story series of motel-like suites, and the layout and amenities have a Southern California look about them. We had nothing official on the agenda this day, so we lounged around the pool that afternoon and shared sea stories.

After a breakfast of very strong coffee, *somvar* and *idli* (spicy chutney and mushy rice), a traditional South Indian dish, we met our car and driver which had been prearranged by the Ministry of External Affairs (Foreign Ministry), and headed off to ISRO and Hindustan Aeronautics Ltd.

Our visit to ISRO was interesting. The Indian Government has a very sophisticated research program directed at putting satellites in stationary orbit above India. We learned, for example, that they had the capability to locate areas in India where ground water was prevalent and also where the vegetation was rapidly dying. This information, if used properly, could support the management of scarce potable water and forest resources. The Indian mindset, however, appeared to be focused on the technology itself and not on solving critical environmental problems. There was no effort to integrate the technology with the problems of the Home Ministry (Interior Ministry). It seemed that the Indians felt a lot of pride about being a member of the club of nations who have the ability to develop very sophisticated technology.

Next we visited Hindustan Aeronautics Ltd. (HAL). During WW II the predecessor to HAL had been a facility built by the U.S. to repair and assemble aircraft, which were being used in the China-Burma-India Theater of the war. After the war the Indian Government took it over and converted the facility to an aircraft production facility. At the time of our visit they were building or conducting concept design on British Tornadoes under license from the UK, small Bell-type helicopters of indigenous design, and a new light combat aircraft, also of indigenous design. We toured the plant and were given a short briefing on future plans. I was especially interested in HAL because it was there that the LM 2500 General Electric gas turbine engines would be fabricated under license to be installed in the Indian Taruntul seagoing patrol craft. East would meet West in India when the U.S. LM2500 would power the Soviet-designed Taruntul! That project was mentioned in the brief, but the international agreements had not yet been signed so no production activity had been started. After a luncheon with the public affairs folks at HAL we departed for the airport for a flight back to New Delhi.

From my point of view spending DAO travel funds on this trip was a good investment. I was able to visit places by piggy-backing or "strap-hanging" on the visit of the Senate staffers—places that I would unlikely have been able to visit on my own, except perhaps for HAL. After the staffers departed, I busily documented the trip and fired off the resulting report to headquarters. About one week later the real fun began. I was looking forward to the next project, wondering what could top the trip to Bombay and Bangalore, when I was called into the Deputy Chief of Mission (DCM's) office. The DCM told me that the Joint Secretary for the Americas Division of the Ministry of Foreign Affairs had formally requested that I meet with him to explain my role in the Bombay and Bangalore trip. I asked what this was all about, and the DCM said he didn't have a clue. The change to the diplomatic note spelled out my role in the visit, and since the Government of India had approved the visit, he could not figure out why such a high-ranking official would summon me to his office. A Joint Secretary is equivalent in rank to an Assistant Secretary of State. The incumbent was in charge of international relations with Mexico, Canada, and the U.S. He had formerly served as the minister counselor (similar to a DCM) in the Indian Embassy in Washington and presumably knew how the U.S. Government was organized and operated. I had met him briefly at a fourth of July party, so I was not walking in on a complete stranger. My recollection was that he thoroughly enjoyed his tour in Washington, and his family was eager to return. I made an appointment to see the Joint Secretary the following week.

There is life after naval service in India.

On the appointed day I took the route to the foreign ministry that passes by all the apartments set aside for members of Parliament. Since Parliament was in session, there was much activity in the area. Clothes just washed were being hung out to dry and some Parliamentarians dressed in *dhotis* were gathered outside their apartments having morning *chai*. The Foreign Ministry was located in South Block, as was Naval Headquarters and the Ministry of Defense, except that the entry to the Foreign Ministry was on the opposite side of the fortress-like building from the Navy entrance. Upon entering, guests were asked to sign in and show their carnet (diplomatic I.D.), and then asked to wait in a musty but elegant anteroom until their point of contact could be reached. After about fifteen minutes, and still puzzled by the purpose of the summons, I was escorted to the Joint Secretary's office.

After a few introductory remarks about the cold winter weather in New Delhi and a cup of *chai*, I was bluntly asked why I was doing the work of the CIA, whose task it was to handle visitors from the U.S. National Foreign Intelligence Community? I retorted that Senate staffers are not from the Intelligence Community. They only conduct oversight with respect to the Community. In addition, the staffers mainly wanted to visit military production facilities here in India, and the military was definitely the bailiwick of the DAO. The Joint Secretary said, "Yes, I know how it works in Washington, but how do I answer the Parliament, whose members will presume you work for the CIA?" "Tell the truth," I said. He retorted, without further explanation, that this would put him in a very difficult position. I explained that what I did was a natural and reasonable thing to do given my responsibilities as a military attaché. I wondered at that point if I was going to be expelled from India because of the Parliament's perception that I was doing something inconsistent with my diplomatic status as a military attaché. I kept thinking to myself, "How can we be having this conversation, when they (the Government of India) officially and in writing gave us permission to make the trip? This question could have been raised before the official notification of approval, and the Joint Secretary would not be in this 'difficult position.'"

Author with makeshift head covering for visiting a Hindu temple.

The issue was not resolved during the meeting. I suppose the Joint Secretary was reacting to questions from Parliament members, and had to go through the motions of calling me in and upbraiding me. I chalked it up to some communist sympathizer either in the Foreign or Defense Ministry who probably put the idea of my not being a "real" attaché into the bonnet of some receptive and Soviet-sympathizing Parliamentarian.

The price I paid for visiting some high-tech centers in India was that I was painted with a brush of suspicion. In my mind it was worth the embarrassment of being chewed out by the foreign ministry. I was not declared *persona non grata* and did not have to uproot my family. The U.S. Government was not embarrassed by the episode. We had followed the prescribed process of submitting a diplomatic note covering the trip and therefore the Government of India could only give me a verbal demarche instead of expulsion. The experience enlightened me about the complexity of Indian attitudes toward American diplomats. At one level it was all right to let U.S. officials see their facilities because of the Indian enjoyment of being thought of as avant-garde or modern. At another there was still the lingering animosity and suspicion of Westerners promoted by the long-standing competition for the "hearts and minds" of the Indians by the U.S. and USSR. It would take some time to undo the effects of the Cold War that was waged hotly in the Third World.

ABOUT THE AUTHOR

Stephen Marrin is a graduate student specializing in intelligence studies at the University of Virginia, and he developed the ideas for this paper as part of his Master's thesis assessing the impact of the CIA's Kent School on analytic quality. He has also participated in CIA's analytic process in three different capacities: in 1996 and 1997 as a leadership analyst for CIA's Office of Near East, South Asia, and Africa; in 1998 as a project assistant for a group in the Office of Transnational Issues; and in 1999 and 2000 as a team leader for a contractor supplying analytical support to the Office of Transnational Issues. As required, this paper has been reviewed by CIA's Publication Review Board, which has no security objection to its dissemination. Their review does not confirm the accuracy of the information nor does it endorse the author's views.

IMPROVING CIA ANALYSIS BY OVERCOMING INSTITUTIONAL OBSTACLES

Stephen Marrin

The accuracy of CIA intelligence analysis depends in part upon an individual analyst's expertise, yet programs implemented to increase this expertise may not be sufficient to increase the accuracy of either an individual's analysis or the institution's output as a whole. Improving analytic accuracy by increasing the expertise of the analyst is not easy to achieve. Even if expertise development programs were to result in greater regional expertise, language capability, or an improved application of methodological tools, the production process itself still takes place within an institutional context that sets parameters for this expertise. The agency's bureaucratic processes and structure can impede an analyst's acquisition and application of additional expertise, preventing the full realization of the potential inherent in expertise development programs. Therefore, any new reform or program intended to improve analytic accuracy by increasing the expertise of its analysts should be supplemented with complementary reforms to bureaucratic processes — and perhaps even organizational structure — so as to increase the likelihood that individual or institutional improvement will occur.

The interplay between analyst and institution within the Intelligence Community remains poorly studied. As Columbia University's Robert Jervis has observed, "perhaps the intelligence community has paid too [little attention] ...to how the community's internal structure and norms might be altered to enable intelligence to be worth listening to."[1] CIA's intelligence production may be subject to improvement, but making that a reality requires a sophisticated understanding of how an analyst operates within the Directorate for Intelligence's [DI's] institutional context. However, empirical verification of this hypothesis is impossible since, as Jervis notes, "[r]igorous measures of the quality of intelligence are lacking" and are insurmountably difficult to create.[2] Under these circumstances, this essay is a conceptual "what-if" exploration into the interplay between the acquisition and application of expertise on three levels: that of the individual, bureaucratic processes, and organizational structure.

THE GOAL: IMPROVING CIA'S ANALYSIS

Improving the accuracy of CIA's finished intelligence products could make an immediate and direct improvement to national security policymaking as well as reduce the frequency and severity of intelligence failures. The CIA's DI—like other intelligence

---

[1] Robert Jervis, "What's Wrong with the Intelligence Process?" *International Journal of Intelligence and Counterintelligence* 1, no. 1 (1986): 41.

[2] Jervis, 30

agencies — ideally provides policymakers with "timely, accurate, and objective" finished intelligence analysis tailored to the needs of the national security policymaker.[3] In the author's experience and observation, a DI analyst interprets the international environment through an information-processing methodology approximating the scientific method to convert raw intelligence data into finished analysis. The traditional "intelligence cycle" describes how an analyst integrates information collected by numerous entities and disseminates this information to policymakers. As William Colby—former Director of Central Intelligence (DCI) and veteran operations officer — notes, "at the center of the intelligence machine lies the analyst, and he is the fellow to whom all the information goes so that he can review it and think about it and determine what it means.[4] Although this model depicts the process in sequential terms, more accurately the analyst is engaged in never-ending conversations with collectors and policymakers over the status of international events and their implications for U.S. policy. As part of this process, intelligence analysts "take the usually fragmentary and inconclusive evidence gathered by the collectors and processors, study it, and write it up in short reports or long studies that meaningfully synthesize and interpret the findings," according to intelligence scholar Loch Johnson.[5]

Intelligence failures of every stripe from the trivial to the vitally important occur every day for a variety of reasons, including the mis-prioritization of collection systems, hasty analysis, and inappropriately applied assumptions. In the mid-1970s Richard Betts effectively settled the academic question of causes of failure by arguing that intelligence failures will be inevitable due to many inherent limitations in the analytic process.[6] Administrators at the Joint Military Intelligence College note that "analysis is subject to many pitfalls — biases, stereotypes, mirror-imaging, simplistic thinking, confusion between cause and effect, bureaucratic politics, group-think, and a host of other human failings."[7] Yet most intelligence failures do not lead to direct negative consequences for the U.S. primarily because the stakes of everyday policymaking are not high, and errors in fact and interpretation can be corrected as the iterative process between intelligence

---

[3] CIA website, "The Role and Mission of the Directorate of Intelligence," URL: *http:// www.odci.gov/cia/di/mission/mission.html.*, accessed October 2001.

[4] William Colby, "Retooling the Intelligence Industry." *Foreign Service Journal* 69, no. 1. (January 1992): 21.

[5] Loch K. Johnson, "Making the Intelligence 'Cycle' Work." *International Journal of Intelligence and Counterintelligence* 1, no. 4 (1986): 11.

[6] Richard K. Betts, "Analysis, War and Decision: Why Intelligence Failures Are Inevitable," *World Politics* 31, no. 1 (October 1978): 61-89.

[7] Ronald D. Garst and Max L. Gross, "On Becoming an Intelligence Analyst." *Defense Intelligence Journal* 6, no. 2 (1997): 48. See also: Richards Heuer, Psychology of Intelligence Analysis (CIA, Center for the Study of Intelligence, 1999); Ralph K. White, "Empathy as an Intelligence Tool," *International Journal of Intelligence and Counterintelligence* 1, no. 1 (Spring 1986): 57-75. Richards Heuer, "Improving Intelligence Analysis: Some Insights on Data, Concepts, And Management in the Intelligence Community" *The Bureaucrat* 8, no. 1 (Winter1979/80): 2-11.

and policy develops. As a result, most failures or inaccuracies are eventually corrected and usually never even noticed. However, sometimes intelligence failure is accompanied by either great policymaker surprise or serious negative consequences for U.S. national security, or both.

The CIA's May 1998 failure to warn American policymakers of India's intentions to test nuclear weapons is an illustration of both kinds of failure. This lapse—widely criticized by foreign policy experts and the press—highlighted intelligence limitations such as the DI's inability to add together all indications of a possible nuclear test and warn top policymakers. According to New York Times correspondent Tim Weiner, these indicators included "the announced intentions of the new Hindu nationalist government to make nuclear weapons part of its arsenal, the published pronouncements of India's atomic weapons commissioner, who said...that he was ready to test if political leaders gave the go-ahead, and ...missile tests by Pakistan that all but dared New Delhi to respond."[8] CIA's inability to integrate these indicators—a failure of analysis—led to charges of "lack of critical thinking and analytic rigor."[9] Admiral David Jeremiah—who headed the official investigation into the failure—concluded that intelligence failed to provide warning in part because analysts "had a mindset that said everybody else is going to work like we work," otherwise known as mirror-imaging.[10] He then "recommended hiring more analysts, improving their training and increasing contact with outside experts to challenge conventional wisdom," according to The Wall Street Journal's Carla Robbins.[11]

CIA's search for ways to improve analytic accuracy and prevent intelligence failure—if successful—could have a positive impact on national security policymaking. The CIA is arguably the centerpiece of the United States' fourteen-agency intelligence community (IC) and "has primary responsibility for all-source intelligence analysis in the [IC] and the preparation of finished national intelligence for the President and his top policymakers," according to former CIA Inspector General Fred Hitz.[12] If CIA analysis does have this kind of central role in influencing policy, improving its accuracy should provide policymakers with the opportunity to create or implement policies that more effectively protect national security and advance national interests.

---

[8]Tim Weiner, "U.S. Blundered on Intelligence, Officials Admit," *New York Times*, 13 May 1998, A14..

[9]James R. Asker, "Same Ol', Same Ol'," *Aviation Week and Space Technology*, 8 June 1998: 21.

[10]CIA website, "Jeremiah News Conference," URL: http://www.cia.gov/cia/public_affairs/press_release/archives/1998/jeremiah.html, accessed October 2001.

[11]Carla Anne Robbins, "Failure to Predict India's Tests Is Tied to Systemwide Intelligence Breakdown," *Wall Street Journal*, 3 June 1998, A8.

[12]For further information on the IC see CIA's website, "United States Intelligence Community," URL: http://www.odci.gov/ic/, accessed October 2001. Also see Frederick P. Hitz, "The Future of American Espionage," *International Journal of Intelligence and Counterintelligence* 13, no. 1 (2000):3.

THE METHOD: INCREASING ANALYTIC EXPERTISE

Improving the capabilities and knowledge of the individual CIA analyst through programs reflecting Admiral Jeremiah's recommendation, is one way to improve the accuracy of intelligence analysis. An analyst's expertise, defined as "the skill of an expert," [13] is a crucial component for the production of accurate intelligence analysis. "In the lexicon of US intelligence professionals, 'analysis' refers to the interpretation by experts of unevaluated ['raw'] information collected by the [IC]," according to Loch Johnson.[14] The presumption is the more "expert" an analyst is the more accurate the resulting interpretation will be. In May 2000, DCI George Tenet described the importance of an analyst's expertise in this manner:

> In our [DI] it is not enough just to make the right call. That takes luck. You have to make the right call for the right reasons. That takes expertise. It is expertise—built up through study and experience—that combines with relevance and rigor to produce something that is very important: insight....[O]ur analysts blend a scholar's mastery of detail with a reporter's sense of urgency and clarity. At its best, the result is insight. And it is insight that wins the confidence of our customers and makes them want to read our publications and listen to our briefings."[15]

Analytic expertise is a multi-faceted concept because CIA uses a complex web of analytic specialties to produce multi-disciplinary analysis. Not hired directly by the CIA or even the DI, most analysts are hired by the individual DI offices and assigned to "groups" that cover specific geographic areas, and are then assigned a functional specialty—"discipline" or "occupation" in DI terminology—such as political, military, economic, leadership, or scientific, technical, and weapons intelligence, according to CIA's website.[16] An analyst's expertise can vary depending on his or her relative degree of regional knowledge, familiarity with disciplinary theory, and with intelligence methods in general:

■ Regional expertise is essentially area studies: a combination of the geography, history, sociology, and political structures of a defined geographic region. The DI's regional offices are responsible for an analyst's regional expertise and develop it by providing access to language training, regional familiarization through university courses, or in-house seminars.

---

[13] Merriam-Webster online, URL: *http://www.m-w.com.*

[14] Loch K. Johnson, "Analysis For a New Age." *Intelligence and National Security* 11, no. 4 (October 1996): 657.

[15] CIA website: "Remarks of the Director of Central Intelligence George J. Tenet at the Dedication of the Sherman Kent School, 4 May 2000," URL: *http://www.cia.gov/cia/public_affairs/ speeches/archives/2000/dci_speech_05052000.html,* accessed October 2001.

[16] On the CIA website, see "Intelligence Disciplines" at URL: *http://www.odci.gov/cia/di/work/ disciplines.html;* also see on the CIA website, "Directorate of Intelligence Organizational Components, Council of Intelligence Occupations," URL: *http://www.cia.gov/cia/di/mission/cioc.html,* accessed October 2001.

■ Disciplinary expertise relates to the theory and practice that underlies the individual analytic occupations. For example, economic, military, political and leadership analysis are built on a bed of theory derived from the academic disciplines of economics, military science, political science, and political psychology, respectively. Disciplinary expertise can be acquired through previous academic coursework, on-the-job experience, or supplementary training.

For the most part each CIA analyst possesses a very small area of direct responsibility defined by a combination of regional area and discipline as they work in country teams with analysts of other disciplines and interact with other regional or disciplinary specialists as the need arises. CIA's small analytic niches create specialists, but their specialties must be re-integrated in order to provide high-level policymakers with a bigger picture that is more accurate and balanced than that arising from the limited perspective or knowledge of the niche analyst. This process of re-integration—known as "coordination" in DI parlance—allows analysts of all kinds to weigh in with their niche expertise on pieces of finished intelligence before they are disseminated. According to CIA analyst Frank Watanabe: "We coordinate to ensure a corporate product and to bring the substantive expertise of others to bear."[17] Accordingly, the bureaucratic norm is for an analyst to make every effort to coordinate a draft with other analysts in related regional or disciplinary accounts prior to submitting the draft to management for editing and dissemination. As a result, whereas the expertise of the primary drafter of the piece usually has primary influence on the accuracy of the final piece, the coordination process exerts a strong influence as well.

Insufficient analytic expertise can cause inaccuracies in intelligence analysis. Robert Jervis points out that "a grav[e] danger lies in not having sufficient expertise about an area or a problem to detect and interpret important trends and developments. To make up for such deficiency, analysts tend to impose on the information the concepts, models, and beliefs that they have derived elsewhere."[18] In addition, in 1991 former DCI Stansfield Turner noted that "[a]nother reason for many of the analytic shortcomings is that our analytical agencies do not have an adequate grasp of the cultures of many countries with which we must deal."[19] Seven years later the CIA failed to provide policymakers with warning of India's nuclear tests for this very reason. To bolster CIA's weaknesses, in 1991 Turner suggested that analysts should be provided with "a better opportunity to attend academic institutions, participate in professional conferences, travel and live abroad, acquire language skills and thus become true experts in their areas."[20] Yet in

---

[17] Frank Watanabe, "Fifteen Axioms for Intelligence Analysts." *Studies in Intelligence*, unclassified edition (1997), URL: *http://www.odci.gov/csi/studies/97unclass/axioms.html*, accessed October 2001.

[18] Jervis, 32.

[19] Stansfield Turner, "Intelligence for A New World Order," *Foreign Affairs* 70, no. 4 (Fall 1991): 163.

[20] Turner, 164.

1998 former CIA officer Robert Steele observed that "[t]he average analyst has 2 to 5 years' experience. They haven't been to the countries they're analyzing. They don't have the language, the historical knowledge, the in-country residence time or the respect of their private-sector peers," as reported by Tim Weiner.[21]

CIA has recently implemented programs to increase analytic expertise. In 2000, then-Deputy Director for Intelligence (DDI) and current Deputy Director of Central Intelligence (DDCI) John McLaughlin created the Sherman Kent School for Intelligence Analysis, which was "designed to give new employees a rigorous, 26-week overview of intelligence analysis"[22] as well as provide training in CIA's analytic disciplines to officers of all levels. In addition, McLaughlin said that CIA is "going all out to achieve greater analytic depth. We are providing incentives for analysts to stay on their accounts longer. We are affording our analysts greater opportunities to travel and to broaden their experience. Because we claim no monopoly on wisdom, we are bringing in outside experts for short tours as scholars-in-residence. We also are encouraging our analysts to expand their contacts with specialists elsewhere in government, in the private sector and in academia."[23]

Increasing expertise may not be sufficient to produce accuracy or prevent failure. As Jervis notes, "experts will [not] necessarily get the right answers. Indeed, the parochialism of those who know all the facts about a particular country that they consider to be unique, but lack the conceptual tools for making sense of much of what they see, is well known."[24] In addition, "[e]ven if the organizational problems...and perceptual impediments to accurate perception were remedied or removed, we could not expect an enormous increase in our ability to predict events" because "(t)he impediments to understanding our world are so great that... intelligence will often reach incorrect conclusions."[25] That is because human cognitive limitations require analysts to simplify reality through the analytic process, but reality simplified is no longer reality. As a result, "even experts can be wrong because their expertise is based on rules which are at best blunt approximations of reality. In the end any analytic judgment will be an approximation of the real world and therefore subject to some amount of error"[26] and analytic inaccuracies—and sometimes intelligence failure—will be

---

[21] Quoted in Tim Weiner, "Naivete at the CIA: Every Nation's Just Another U.S.," *New York Times Week in Review*, 7 June 1998, 5.

[22] Vernon Loeb, "CIA's Analysis Becomes Transnational," *Washington Post Online*, 2 April 2001, URL: *http://www.washingtonpost.com/ac2/wp-dyn?pagename=article&node=&contentId=A16925-2001Mar30*

[23] CIA website, "Remarks of the Deputy Director..., Princeton," URL: *http://www.cia.gov/cia/public_affairs/speeches/ddci_speech_03092001.html*

[24] Jervis, 31-32.

[25] Jervis, 28, 30.

[26] Stephen Marrin, "Complexity is in the Eye of the Beholder," DI Discussion Database (an internal CIA bulletin board), 6 May 1997.

inevitable. Therefore, although increasing expertise is a goal, it cannot be the only goal for increasing DI capabilities.

Nevertheless, the DI leadership has created multiple expertise development initiatives to counter perceptions of analytic inadequacy and increase the DI's core capability — its analytic expertise. The unanswered question is whether the analyst can acquire and apply relevant expertise within the institutional constraints of the DI.

FIRST INTERVENING FACTOR: BUREAUCRATIC PROCESSES

Bureaucratic processes can impede the acquisition or application of expertise gained in expertise development programs, thereby limiting any potential improvement in overall analytic accuracy. The DI is a bureaucracy, and like every bureaucracy creates "standard operating procedures" (SOPs) which are necessary for efficient functioning but over time usually prove to be rigid in implementation.[27] As former DDI Doug MacEachin noted in 1994: "We have all been a part of what has been good and of what needs changing. Some of the practices needing change came into being as the unforeseen result of efforts undertaken for sound constructive reasons, judged by participants at the time to have been fully valid and usually aimed at correcting deficiencies of the time. But collectively, with time and bureaucratic evolution, they turned out to be counterproductive."[28] Some of the DI's SOPs prevent analysts from applying the tradecraft standards and other forms of expertise learned elsewhere. Jack Davis, a former DI officer and analytic methodologist, observed that "examples of what MacEachin would label as poorly substantiated analysis are still seen (after training). Clearly, ongoing vigilance is needed to keep such analysis from finding its way into DI products."[29] Such vigilance includes assessing the bureaucratic context for obstacles preventing tradecraft application.

Analysts must have the opportunity to apply newly acquired expertise back at their desks in the DI for any improvement to result. However, if analysts do not have the opportunity to apply this expertise, it will likely wither for lack of practice. The DI produces many types of finished intelligence—some reportorial, some analytical, and some estimative—to meet policymakers' varying needs for information. In addition to daily updates on developments worldwide, policymakers and their staffs also use information and analyses when crafting policy and monitoring its implementation. Obstacles to the development of expertise appear when shorter product types are emphasized over longer more

---

[27] If bureaucracies stultify good ideas by turning them into "standard operating procedures" regardless of situation — as Graham Allison's organizational process model in his *Essence of Decision* implies — then a bureaucracy is forever in a state of flux, somewhere along the pendulum from one bureaucratized extreme to the other.

[28] Douglas J. MacEachin and others, *The Tradecraft of Analysis: Challenge and Change in the CIA* (Washington, DC: Consortium for the Study of Intelligence, 1994), 1.

[29] Jack Davis, "Improving Intelligence Analysis at CIA: Dick Heuer's Contribution to Intelligence Analysis," in "Introduction" to *Psychology of Intelligence Analysis*, Richards J. Heuer (Washington, DC: Center for the Study of Intelligence, 1999), xix.

research-oriented ones. Short turnaround products—including daily updates known as "current" intelligence—have at times been emphasized over other products for their greater relevancy to policymakers, but this emphasis at the same time has reduced the expertise of the DI writ large because they require different kinds of mental operations that reduce the scope and scale of an analyst's research and knowledge. Robert Jervis once observed that "the informal norms and incentives of the intelligence community often form what Charles Perrow has called 'an error-inducing system.' That is, interlocking and supporting habits of the community systematically decrease the likelihood that careful and penetrating intelligence analyses will be produced and therefore make errors extremely likely."[30] Bureaucratic processes can contribute to the creation of this kind of "error-inducing system."

The Swinging Pendulum

For much of the DI's history, analysts acquired expertise by writing long reports. As former CIA officer Arthur Hulnick notes: "a great deal of research was being done, but ...much of it was done to enable the analyst to speak authoritatively on a current issue, rather than for publication."[31] Loch Johnson agrees, saying that "[t]he preparation of longer reports...is important, too, as ... a vital learning experience for analysts."[32] He adds that "[I]ntellectually most satisfying to the intelligence analyst is the full-blown research project, for it allows more room for the tracing of nuances. ... Under the Reagan administration, the [DI] established a research program...[in which] each of the ten [DI] offices...was told to redouble its efforts to produce solid research papers. In one nine-month period, more than 900 such reports were in progress... .[A]s Gates has claimed, 'the CIA is the only place where long-range research on national security issues is being done—two, five, ten, twenty years down the road. The Department of State Planning Staff conducts this kind of research only sporadically.'"[33]

By the early 1990s, however, long papers had become bureaucratized. In a 1993 article, former analyst Jay Young argued that "the needs of the policy-maker too often get lost in the time-consuming, self-absorbed and corrosive intelligence research production process. The DI's research program is run with the same rigid attention to production quotas as any five-year plan in the old USSR. ... This fixation on numerical production leads managers to keep analysts working away on papers whose relevance may be increasingly questionable. ... In short, too much of the Agency's longer-term research is untimely, on subjects of marginal importance and chock-full of fuzzy judgments."[34] He went on to

---

[30] Jervis, 34.

[31] Arthur S. Hulnick, "Managing Intelligence Analysis: Strategies for Playing the End Game," *International Journal of Intelligence and Counterintelligence* 2, no. 3 (1988): 322-323.

[32] Loch K. Johnson, "Analysis For a New Age," 665.

[33] Loch K. Johnson, "Making the Intelligence "Cycle" Work," 6-7.

[34] Jay T. Young, "US Intelligence Assessment in a Changing World: The Need for Reform," *Intelligence and National Security* 8, no. 2 (April 1993): 129, 134.

advocate a reduction in the number of long papers published each year. In short, although longer papers helped develop analytic expertise, bureaucratic tendencies had made their production increasingly irrelevant to policymakers.

In response to such criticisms, DI managers dictated that relevancy required shorter papers. In 1994, then-DDI Doug MacEachin limited "most DI analytical papers ... to 3 to 7 pages, including graphics and illustrations."[35] Shorter reports made the DI's analytical output more useful for policymakers, but analysts acquired less expertise on each topic. As a result, while the papers were more targeted, they contained fewer insights for the policymaker. Predictably, complaints then arose that the DI lacked the expertise necessary to do quality analysis. According to former DI analyst John Gentry in 1995:

> For reasons that heavily reflect its changing internal culture, CIA has begun to think much more myopically. It even claims now that it is emphasizing "tactical" projects and largely eliminated "strategic" work. In the DI, these terms are new ones for what formerly were "current intelligence" and "research," respectively... The change is major and is formal policy...In other words, CIA has given up its former mission of trying to develop the analytic expertise and the information assets to forecast another Pearl Harbor in favor of collecting information to serve the analytic priority of drafting the short, pithy pieces for the National Intelligence Daily (NID) and other current intelligence publications...This change is enormous — and it is enormously irresponsible. ...[T]he failure to devote resources to long-term collection and to the development and maintenance of analytical expertise risks major surprises — and major intelligence failures — in the future.[36]

By 1997, DI management had admitted that the pendulum had swung too far and they were making efforts to address the decreased level of expertise. In 1997, then-DDI John McLaughlin noted that the DI's recent "impressive record of supporting the current intelligence needs of senior policymakers" made "an enormous claim on our personnel and resources" and the DI was "trying to balance the need for current support against the need to look ahead."[37] Since then the DI has emphasized acquisition of expertise, and funded opportunities for analysts to gain it by arguing that "[a]nother priority for intelligence analysis is to deliver a product that adds context and meaning to the raw intelligence. ...

---

[35] Center for Security Policy, "'Say It Ain't So, Jim': Impending Reorganization of CIA Looks Like Suppression, Politicizing of Intelligence," Publication No. 94-D74, 15 July 1994, URL: *http://www.security-policy.org/papers/1994/94-D74.html*, accessed October 2001.

[36] John A.Gentry, "A Framework for Reform of the U.S. Intelligence Community," 6 June 1995, remarks prepared for presentation to congressional intelligence committees, presented by the Federal of American Scientists at URL: *http://www.fas.org/irp/gentry/*, accessed October 2001.

[37] John E. McLaughlin, "New Challenges and Priorities for Analysis," *Defense Intelligence Journal* 6, no. 2 (Fall 1997): 17.

One of the ways to stay relevant is to build and maintain subject matter expertise, continuity, and depth within the analytical ranks."[38]

Losing Expertise to Gain Relevance

The swing of the pendulum that emphasizes policymaker relevance over analytic depth causes the DI to produce a large amount of current intelligence that prevents the acquisition and application of analytic expertise. Many analysts are facile data interpreters able to integrate large volumes of new information with existing knowledge, and interpret—based on underlying conceptual constructs—the significance of the new data in terms of its implications for U.S. foreign policymaking. This process provides policymakers with exactly what they are looking for from intelligence analysis. However, if provided with minimal time in which to integrate and process the information, the intelligence analyst by necessity cuts corners. When the DI emphasizes intelligence "on-demand," analysts meet the much shorter deadlines by reducing the scope and scale of their research as well as sidestepping the more laborious tradecraft procedures by not rigorously scrutinizing assumptions or comparing working hypotheses to competing explanations. Many times current intelligence analysis consists of a single hypothesis—derived within the first hour of the tasking—that the analyst intuitively believes provides the best explanation for the data. Current intelligence as a product has a lesser chance of being accurate because it lacks the self-conscious rigor that tradecraft entails even though it is the best that can be done under the press of quick deadlines.

The production of a single piece of current intelligence has limited effect on expertise because it draws on the knowledge and tools that an analyst has developed through training and prior analysis. However, if over time the analyst does not have the time to think, learn, or integrate new information with old to create new understandings, knowledge of facts and events may increase but the ability to interpret these events accurately decreases.

In a production environment attuned to the policymaker's current need for information, analysts will fail to apply the newly acquired expertise and instead will fall back to providing intuitive rather than structured analysis. Intelligence scholar Robert Folker observed that in his interviews of intelligence analysts a "repeated complaint was the analyst's lack of time to devote to thoughtful intelligence analysis. In a separate interview at CIA it was revealed that [intelligence analysts]... spend little time or effort conducting analysis."[39] Therefore, the effectiveness of expertise development programs in improving analytic accuracy may depend in part on whether the CIA is able to redress the overemphasis on short-term analysis. Balancing the swinging pendulum is easier to recom-

---

[38] McLaughlin, 18.

[39] Robert D. Folker, *Intelligence Analysis in Theater Joint Intelligence Centers: An Experiment in Applying Structured Methods*, Occasional Paper Number Seven (Washington, DC: Joint Military Intelligence College, January 2000), 12.

mend than to do since production of both extremes—long-term research and current intelligence support—may be necessary.

A Structural Fix?

If the DI remains true to form, at some time in the future the pendulum will swing too far toward knowledge-creation, papers will become longer and less relevant to policymakers. Perhaps there is a way to diagnose more accurately the cause of this swing and find a middle-ground that balances the trade-offs. The answer, however, does not lie in directives from the top that emphasize the utility or desirableness of one product type over another. These will likely just be encapsulated into the DI's SOPs and move the pendulum too far in the opposite direction. Instead, if CIA were to bifurcate its intelligence production system to specialize both in long-term research and current intelligence support, it would side-step the trade-offs between timeliness and accuracy that ultimately cause the pendulum to swing, and make the best use of any expertise-development program. Underlying this suggestion is a more strategic and nuanced approach to human resources management than CIA currently uses.

Just as there are different kinds of intelligence products requiring different levels of analytic ability, individual analysts possess varying cognitive strengths and weaknesses. As a senior DI analyst noted in an internal computer discussion in 1997, there may be two types of cognitive preferences — not "mutually exclusive"—that differentiate one kind of analyst from another: "Some people are better at...a broad range of issues, areas, and disciplines. These make the best current intelligence analysts because they generally are quick to learn an account. ... In simple terms, these are the people who are good at crafting a coherent story from a jumble of seemingly disconnected parts. ... Becoming an expert at this kind of analysis requires a great deal of experience. ... An expert of this type needs to continuously cast a net over a greater range of evidence and then relate it." He then goes on to add that it is better if this kind of analyst has experience on multiple accounts. Then he contrasts this expert generalist to "the other type of expert analyst...who concentrates on learning as much as possible about their chosen subject, area, or discipline. These are our specialists. They do the basic research, build our corporate knowledge base, and concentrate on depth rather than breadth. In the old days in the DDI, managers used to call these analysts the investors. They put money in the bank account which the current intelligence analysts draw out to spend. ... University study, technical training, language proficiency, and several years on an account are a necessity for developing the type of analytical expertise we need for our specialists."[40]

The DI appears to be remarkably blind to differentiation in both analysis and analysts, perhaps because it assigns tasks to "analysts" and equates the output with "analysis." As a result, "[w]e do not and never have used the term 'analysis' rigorously in the [IC]" according to Robert Bovey, formerly a special assistant to a DCI.[41] Robert Jervis

---

[40]CIA officer, "Two Types of Expert Analyst," DI Discussion Database, 28 March 1997.

illustrated the problems of equating the two in 1988 by arguing that "most political analysis would better be described as political reporting" and that instead of following an analytical approach "the analyst is expected to summarize the recent reports from the field—"cable-gisting." ... [T]he reporting style is not analytical—there are few attempts to dig much beneath the surface of events, to look beyond the next few weeks, to consider alternative explanations for the events, or to carefully marshal evidence that could support alternative views."[42] Jervis correctly differentiated the analytical intelligence product from its non-analytic cousin, but failed to distinguish between the analysts best suited for each. The DI — instead of differentiating between analysts — uses a one-size-fits-all recruitment, placement, training, and promotion strategy, and for the most part views analysts as interchangeable. As a result it has perennially had difficulty creating an appropriate mix of analytic abilities and skills for intelligence production when an issue or crisis develops. In particular, over time the shift in expertise corresponding to a preference for longer papers or shorter more current pieces is especially noticeable.

An intelligence production system bifurcated by product type would likely eliminate many of the problems inherent in the current system. In the early 1950s CIA intelligence production was organized by product type. The Office of Research and Reports produced basic intelligence, the Office of National Estimates provided forward-looking estimates, and the Office of Current Intelligence "produce[d] the President's daily intelligence publication," [43] according to the Agency's website. Resurrecting an Office of Current Intelligence to handle immediate requests and an Office of Research and Reports to do longer-term analytic papers could provide a self-selection mechanism useful for targeting an individual's cognitive strengths at the policymakers' intelligence needs. This structure would not promote the loss of expertise because different kinds of expertise would be applied to appropriate product types. However, this organizational structure would also require trade-offs-examined below—that would reduce regional expertise on the margins at the same time as it would allow the experts to increase theirs.

SECOND INTERVENING FACTOR:
ORGANIZATIONAL STRUCTURE

The DI's organizational structure also influences which kind of analyst expertise is acquired and applied in finished intelligence products. Political scientist Thomas Hammond argues that organizational structure impacts analytic output. He employs information-flow models to demonstrate that—given the same information—one group of intelligence analysts organized by discipline would produce different analytic output than another group organized by region. He also concludes that it is impossible to

---

[41] Robert Bovey, "The Quality of Intelligence Analysis." *American Intelligence Journal* 3, no. 4 (Winter 1980-81): 7.

[42] Jervis, 34-35.

[43] CIA website, "Key Events in DI History," URL: *http://www.cia.gov/cia/di/history/*, accessed October 2001.

design a structure that does not impact output.[44] If we accept his argument, then organizational structure always affects internal information flows, and likely outputs as well. Theoretically, therefore, an organizational structure divided along disciplinary lines will accentuate learning of political, economic, military, or leadership methodologies through constant, interactive contact and awareness of the projects of other analysts.

However, regional or country knowledge is sacrificed due to the lack of such contact. In an office structured along geographic lines, the emphasis will be reversed. The 1998 India intelligence failure provides a good illustration of how organization can affect expertise. Prior to the 1996 creation of the National Imagery and Mapping Agency, imagery analysts had been distributed, by affiliation at least, throughout the Intelligence Community.[45] According to former CIA analyst Melvin Goodman, "the consolidation of all analysis of satellite imagery in (NIMA)...contributed to the intelligence failure. By placing all analysis of imagery inside the Department of Defense...there would be a minimum of the critical cross-discipline analysis required for difficult regional problems such as the political and military frictions in South Asia."[46] This episode may be considered an illustration of how trade-offs in expertise inherent in organizational structure can affect the DI as well.

Over the past 50 years the DI has been structured by product type, by discipline, and by region. From approximately the early 1960s to 1981, the DI was structured primarily by discipline with political, economic, military, and leadership offices each subdivided by geography. In 1981 "(a) (DI)-wide reorganization...shuffled most analysts and created geographically based, or "regional" offices out of the previous organization."[47] According to former CIA officer Arthur Hulnick: "These [new] offices combined political, economic, military, and other kinds of research under "one roof," thus making more detailed analytic research feasible. After some grumbling, the new offices began to turn out the in-depth products consumers had been seeking, while still providing current intelligence materials."[48] This integration of analytic disciplines in regional offices provided a more productive interpretation of the forces at work within a target country or region but also negatively affected the DI's ability to maintain disciplinary knowledge.

The 1995 dismantling of the DI's Office of Leadership Analysis (LDA) provides a good case study into the trade-offs between disciplinary and regional expertise resulting from differing organizational arrangements.[49] Since at least 1963 the CIA has consolidated biographic information on foreign leaders, and over time the value of leadership analysis as a complement to political, economic, and military analysis became evident.[50]

---

[44] Thomas H. Hammond, "Agenda Control, Organizational Structure, and Bureaucratic Politics" *American Journal of Political Science* 30, no. 2 (May 1986): 379-420.

[45] CIA website, "National Imagery and Mapping Agency," URL: *http://www.cia.gov/ic/ nima.html*, accessed October 2001.

[46] Melvin A. Goodman, "US Intelligence Failure Shows Need for Reform," *Christian Science Monitor*, 18 May 1998, URL: http://www.csmonitor.com/durable/1998/05/18/p11s1.htm, accessed October 2001.

[47] Gentry, URL: *http://www.fas.org/irp/gentry/*, accessed October 2001.

[48] Hulnick, 323.

Analysis grounded in the theory of political psychology provided insight into a leader's behavior above and beyond the limited biographic scope of a leadership profile.[51]   LDA was thus created to develop and consolidate the discipline of leadership analysis and put it on a near-equal basis with the other established analytic disciplines. However, in 1994, then-DDI Doug MacEachin reorganized LDA — the only disciplinary office left — out of existence as part of "downsizing the DI."[52] Political factors may have played a part in this decision. The Clinton Administration's Haiti policy was greatly complicated by partisan opposition in the wake of a leaked leadership profile produced by LDA that questioned the psychological stability of Jean Bertrand Aristide.[53] In any case, LDA's elimination had an impact on the expertise of the DI's leadership analysts.

The regional offices swallowed LDA as its component units were assigned to the relevant regional office. Some regional offices kept leadership analysts together as a team so as to maintain the disciplinary knowledge developed in LDA. Other offices broke leadership teams apart and assigned individual analysts to join multi-disciplinary country teams. The distribution of what had previously been centralized knowledge of analytic tools, specialized product formats, and disciplinary theory throughout the DI meant that new leadership analysts were not well trained in their discipline. These new analysts relied solely on the fast-dissipating knowledge of the handful of former LDA officers who happened to be assigned to their team or issue. In addition, actual physical co-location did not occur for months — and in some cases years — due to lack of space in CIA's overcrowded headquarters building. As a result of being "out of sight, out of mind," leadership analysts were frequently not informed of ongoing projects, briefings, and meetings, and such incidents had a negative impact on the finished analytical product. When leadership analysts were not included in briefings, the DI risked failing to keep its consumers fully informed of both leadership dynamics and changes within the country or region. In addition, products published and disseminated without coordination at times contained factual errors such as the wrong names or positions for foreign government officials, or distortions in analysis due to the lack of leadership analyst input. However, once re-organization occurred, regional counterpart analysts became team members, and after a shaking-out period began to incorporate leadership analyst contributions into their products more easily. In fact, the close interaction with other members of the regional team led to a better incorporation of leadership analysis into regional products than had occurred during the heyday

---

[49]The information herein on LDA is derived from personal experience as a leadership analyst from 1996 to 1998.

[50]CIA website, "Key Events In DI History," URL: *http://www.odci.gov/cia/di/history/ index.html*, accessed October 2001.

[51]Thomas Omestad, "Psychology and the CIA: Leaders on the Couch," *Foreign Policy* 95 (Summer 1994): 105-122.

[52]CIA website, "Key Events In DI History," URL: *http://www.odci.gov/cia/di/history/ index.html*, accessed October 2001.

[53]Center for Security Policy, URL: *http://www.security-policy.org/papers/1994/94-D74.htm*l, accessed October 2001.

of LDA. Therefore, the elimination of a leadership analysis-based office resulted in both increased incorporation of leadership analysis and insight into the regional teams' products, and decreased corporate knowledge and expertise in leadership analysis as a discipline. The same occurred for the other disciplines when their respective offices were eliminated in 1981.

PUTTING THE PIECES TOGETHER AGAIN

By the mid-1990s DI analysts were realizing that while multi-disciplinary analysis on country teams made for better integration of disciplines, it also led to the dissipation of disciplinary knowledge. Former LDA analysts' efforts to sustain their hold on disciplinary knowledge triggered similar efforts by political, economic and military analysts to both sustain and reconstruct occupational-specific knowledge. Without the framework of structural organization to bind each discipline together, over time they had each grown apart.

To rectify this loss of disciplinary expertise, in 1997 the DI created the "senior-level" Council of Intelligence Occupations (CIOC) with the initial intent of disciplinary "workforce strategic planning...in the areas of recruitment, assignments, and training" as well as "identify[ing] core skills and standards for expertise in the [DI]."[54] In practice, CIOC became a home for senior analysts interested in learning and teaching their discipline's methodologies. They "establish[ed] a professional development program for all DI employees that provides explicit proficiency criteria at each level so that everyone can see the knowledge, skills, and experiences required for advancement within each occupation or across occupations."[55] All this was done—according to the CIA website—"so that the DI has the expertise needed to provide value-added all-source analysis to its customers."[56] CIOC emphasized disciplinary training as a method to achieve this goal. As the CIA's website notes, "(t)he Council views learning and skills development as an essential part of work and the means whereby employees can respond to changes in customer priorities and the external environment."[57] In 2000, CIOC was disbanded although its training functions have been incorporated into the DI's Kent School and its other knowledge has been distributed elsewhere within the DI.

There may be no easy solution to the expertise trade-offs inherent in organizational structure. By definition, the structure will create synergies in the areas emphasized but the opportunity cost of doing so means losing the synergies in other areas. At bottom this

---

[54] McLaughlin, 18.

[55] CIA website, "Directorate of Intelligence Organizational Components, Council of Intelligence Occupations," URL: *http://www.cia.gov/cia/di/mission/cioc.html*, accessed October 2001.

[56] CIA website, "Directorate of Intelligence Organizational Components, Council of Intelligence Occupations," URL: *http://www.cia.gov/cia/di/mission/cioc.html*, accessed October 2001.

[57] CIA website, "Directorate of Intelligence Organizational Components, Council of Intelligence Occupations," URL: *http://www.cia.gov/cia/di/mission/cioc.html*, accessed October 2001.

is a prioritization issue: the organizational structure should reflect the dynamic that the DI leadership believes will most directly benefit its policymaker consumers. Establishing secondary institutions like CIOC or disciplinary training through the Kent School to bolster the lost expertise may be the only way to preserve knowledge that otherwise would be lost.

TO THE FUTURE

Expertise-development programs that create the potential to improve overall analytic accuracy—such as formal training in methodologies, regions, disciplines, or languages, or informal training resulting from greater overseas experience — do not provide much in the way of improvement if in fact the DI's business practices prevent application of this hard-earned expertise. CIA's leaders should continue to pursue ways to increase analyst expertise, for they could contribute to increased analytic accuracy. Yet at the same time the DI must adapt its practices to leverage the potential improvements of these programs if the CIA is to provide its policymaking customers with the intelligence they need now and in the future. The creation of a bifurcated production process might remove an impediment preventing acquisition and application of expertise, but other reforms may be necessary as well.

The CIA was created in the wake of the Japanese attack on Pearl Harbor to coordinate and integrate intelligence information and provide strategic warning should any foe of the United States choose to attack. With respect to the September 2001 attacks on the U.S. — it is still too soon to determine whether the CIA's failure to provide specific warning lay in organizational inefficiencies, collection gaps, analytic missteps, or in some combination of the three. Regardless, improvements in intelligence analysis must occur so as to provide policymakers with warning of any potential future attacks while preventing surprises on issues of national security importance. Managing the DI so that it can produce accurate intelligence will require an accurate assessment of the DI's current capabilities, an understanding of its limitations, and creative approaches to overcome them. Current DI business practices entail tradeoffs that prevent full actualization of the DI's potential. Perhaps through serious study the constraints that the DI's working environment imposes on analytic expertise will be understood and overcome. As Robert Jervis declares, "(w)e will never be able to do as well as we would like, but this does not mean that we cannot do better than we are doing now."[58]

BIBLIOGRAPHY

Asker, James R. "Same Ol', Same Ol'." *Aviation Week and Space Technology*, 8 June 1998: 21.

Betts, Richard K. "Analysis, War and Decision: Why Intelligence Failures Are Inevitable. *World Politics* 31, no. 1 (October 1978): 61-89.

Betts, Richard K. "Policy-Makers and Intelligence Analysts: Love, Hate or Indifference?"'

---

[58] Jervis, 30.

Intelligence and National Security 3, no. 1 (January 1988): 184-189.

Bovey, Robert. "The Quality of Intelligence Analysis." *American Intelligence Journal* 3 no. 4 (Winter 1980-81): 6-11.

Center for Security Policy. "'Say It Ain't So, Jim': Impending Reorganization of CIA Looks Like Suppression, Politicizing of Intelligence." Publication No. 94-D74, 15 July 1994. Available at URL: *http://www.security-policy.org/papers/1994/94-D74.html*. Accessed October 2001.

CIA officer. "Two Types of Expert Analyst," DI Discussion Database, 28 March 1997.

CIA website. "Directorate of Intelligence Organizational Components, Council of Intelligence Occupations," URL: *http://www.cia.gov/cia/di/mission/cioc.html*. Accessed October 2001.

CIA website. "Intelligence Disciplines." URL: *http://www.odci.gov/cia/di/work/disciplines.html*. Accessed October 2001.

CIA website. "Jeremiah News Conference." URL: *http://www.cia.gov/cia/public_affairs/press_release/archives/1998/jeremiah.html*. Accessed October 2001.

CIA website. "Key Events In DI History." URL: *http://www.odci.gov/cia/di/history/index.html*. Accessed October 2001.

CIA website. "National Imagery and Mapping Agency." URL: *http://www.cia.gov/ic/nima.html*. Accessed October 2001.

CIA website. "Remarks of the Deputy Director of Central Intelligence John E. McLaughlin at the Conference on CIA's Analysis of the Soviet Union, 1947-1991, Princeton University 9 March 2001." URL: *http://www.cia.gov/cia/public_affairs/speeches/ddci_speech_03092001.html*. Accessed October 2001.

CIA website. "Remarks of the Director of Central Intelligence George J. Tenet at the of the Sherman Kent School, 4 May 2000." URL: *http://www.cia.gov/cia/public_affairs/speeches/archives/2000/dci_speech_05052000.html*. Accessed October 2001.

CIA website. "The Role and Mission of the Directorate of Intelligence." URL: *http://www.odci.gov/cia/di/mission/mission.html*. Accessed October 2001.

Colby, William. "Retooling the Intelligence Industry." *Foreign Service Journal* 69, no. 1 (January 1992): 21-25.

Davis, Jack. "Improving Intelligence Analysis at CIA: Dick Heuer's Contribution to Intelligence Analysis," in "Introduction" to *Psychology of Intelligence Analysis*, Richards J. Heuer, Jr. (Washington, DC: Center for the Study of Intelligence, 1999), xix.

Folker, Robert D. *Intelligence Analysis in Theater Joint Intelligence Centers: An Experiment in Applying Structured Methods*, Occasional Paper Number Seven (Washington, DC: Joint Military Intelligence College, January 2000).

Garst, Ronald D and Max L. Gross. "On Becoming an Intelligence Analyst." *Defense Intelligence Journal* 6, no. 2 (1997): 47-59.

Gentry, John A. "A Framework for Reform of the U.S. Intelligence Community." Remarks prepared for presentation to congressional intelligence committees, 6 June 1995. Available on the Federation of American Scientists webpage at URL: *http://www.fas.org/irp/gentry/*. Accessed October 2001.

Goodman, Melvin A. "US Intelligence Failure Shows Need for Reform." *Christian Science Monitor*, 18 May 1998, 11. URL: *http://www.csmonitor.com/durable/1998/05/18/p11s1.htm*. Accessed October 2001.

Hammond, Thomas H. "Agenda Control, Organizational Structure, and Bureaucratic Politics." *American Journal of Political Science* 30, no. 2 (May 1986): 379-420.

Heuer, Richards J. Jr. "Improving Intelligence Analysis: Some Insights on Data, Concepts and Management in the Intelligence Community." *The Bureaucrat* 8, no. 1 (Winter 1979/80):2-11.

Hitz, Frederick P. "The Future of American Espionage." *International Journal of Intelligence and Counterintelligence* 13, no. 1 (2000): 1-20.

Hulnick, Arthur S. "Managing Intelligence Analysis: Strategies for Playing the End Game." *International Journal of Intelligence and Counterintelligence* 2, no. 3 (1988): 321-343.

Jervis, Robert. "What's Wrong with the Intelligence Process?" *International Journal of Intelligence and Counterintelligence* 1, no. 1 (1986): 28-41.

Johnson, Loch K. "Analysis For a New Age." *Intelligence and National Security* 11, no. 4 (October 1996): 657-671.

_____. "Making the Intelligence 'Cycle' Work." *International Journal of Intelligence and Counterintelligence* 1, no. 4 (1986): 1-23.

Loeb, Vernon. "CIA's Analysis Becomes Transnational." *Washington Post Online*, 2 April 2001. URL: *http://www.washingtonpost.com/ac2/wp-dyn?pagename=article&node=&contentId=A16925-2001Mar30*

MacEachin, Douglas J. and others. *The Tradecraft of Analysis: Challenge and Change in the CIA*. Washington, DC: Consortium for the Study of Intelligence, 1994.

McLaughlin, John E. "New Challenges and Priorities for Analysis." *Defense Intelligence Journal* 6, no. 2 (Fall 1997): 11-21.

Marrin, Stephen. "Complexity is in the Eye of the Beholder," DI Discussion Database, 6 May 1997.

Omestad, Thomas. "Psychology and the CIA: Leaders on the Couch." *Foreign Policy* 95 (Summer 1994): 105-122.

Robbins, Carla Anne. "Failure to Predict India's Tests Is Tied to Systemwide Intelligence Breakdown." *Wall Street Journal*, 3 June 1998, A8.

Turner, Stansfield. "Intelligence for A New World Order." *Foreign Affairs* 70, no. 4 (Fall 1991): 150-166.

Watanabe, Frank. "Fifteen Axioms for Intelligence Analysts." *Studies in Intelligence*. Unclassified edition, 1997. Available at URL: *http://www.odci.gov/csi/studies/97unclass/axioms.html*. Accessed October 2001.

Weiner, Tim. "Naivete at the CIA: Every Nation's Just Another U.S." *New York Times: Week in Review*, 7 June 1998, 5.

Weiner, Tim. "U.S. Blundered on Intelligence, Officials Admit." *New York Times*, 13 May 1998, A1, A14.

White, Ralph K. "Empathy As an Intelligence Tool." *International Journal of Intelligence and Counterintelligence* 1, no. 1 (Spring 1986): 57-75.

Young, Jay T. "US Intelligence Assessment in a Changing World: The Need for Reform." *Intelligence and National Security* 8, no. 2 (April 1993): 125-139.

ABOUT THE AUTHOR

Lt Col Tom Garin, an Air Force officer assigned to the National Reconnaissance Office (NRO), arrived at the Joint Military Intelligence College in September 1999 to occupy the General Thomas S. Moorman, Jr. Chair for National Reconnaissance Systems. He has taught graduate-level core and elective courses on missiles and space systems, structured techniques for intelligence analysis, and research methodologies, as well as an undergraduate core course on space systems. Prior to this post, Lt Col Garin was Chief, Organizational Development at the NRO. There, he used a balanced scorecard approach to link human resource policies with the overall NRO mission. He also worked part-time for Vice President Gore's National Performance Review on a performance measurement benchmarking study team to help government agencies prepare for the Government Performance and Results Act. In addition, he completed special projects as directed by the Assistant Secretary of the Air Force for Space.

Lt Col Garin received a B.S. in Operations Research (OR) from the United States Air Force Academy in 1982, a M.S. in OR from the Air Force Institute of Technology in March 1990, and a Master of Public Administration from the University of Southern California (USC) in May 2001. He is currently in the Doctorate of Public Administration program at USC.

APPRAISING BEST PRACTICES IN DEFENSE INTELLIGENCE ANALYSIS

Thomas A. Garin, Lt Col, USAF

An adaptable organization is one that has the capacity for internal change in response to external conditions. To be adaptable, organizations must be able to learn. Organizations can learn by monitoring their environment, relating this information to internal norms, detecting any deviations from these norms, and correcting discrepancies. The National Foreign Intelligence Community at large learns by collecting necessary information, analyzing the information, and disseminating it to users who in turn hold the option to influence collection decisions. A telling aspect of any knowledge organization is the way in which it manages its information.

Knowledge management can equip intelligence organizations for the fast-paced, high-technology information age. By building upon the best aspects of total quality management, and observing the criteria for performance excellence adopted for the Baldrige National Quality Program, managers can theoretically lead professionals to work together effectively as a group in a situation in which their dealings with one another affect their common welfare. In this paper, Baldrige criteria guide an "insider's" exploration of how a set of senior intelligence officers of the Defense Intelligence Agency do intelligence analysis.[1]

STUDY DESIGN

The DIA is expected to ensure the satisfaction of the full range of foreign military and military-related intelligence requirements of defense organizations, UN Coalition Forces, and non-defense consumers, as appropriate. Specifically, DIA supports: (1) joint military operations in peacetime, crisis, contingency, and combat; (2) service weapons acquisition; and (3) defense policymaking. In the past fifteen years, several analysis and production units within DIA have received prestigious awards demonstrating the confidence and appreciation that senior U.S. leaders have in the agency's performance. On the basis of these observations, a case could be made that DIA has become a world-class organization for meeting U.S. military intelligence requirements. Clearly, the DIA is a worthy organization to examine for evidence of how quality intelligence analysis can be carried out.

---

[1] The three essential characteristics of operations research are (1) systems orientation, (2) use of interdisciplinary teams, and (3) adaptation of the scientific method. The Baldrige criteria provide a similar function for assessing information organizations. From a systems perspective, the Baldrige criteria focus on a leadership triad and a results triad. Activity by leadership affects results and the results, in turn, affect the future activity of leadership. From a team perspective, the Baldrige criteria focus on the multiple lens of leadership, the customers or consumers, and the analysts to gain a complete understanding of its operations. Lastly, the Baldrige criteria focus on information and analysis, emphasizing a fact-based, scientific approach, to serve as a foundation for the performance management system.

A Typical Office

A typical analysis office consists of a manager, the senior intelligence officer (SIO), analysts, liaison officers, and administration/technical support staff. The manager handles a set of processes common to many organizations such as planning, organizing, staffing, directing, coordinating, reporting, and budgeting. The SIO is a senior analyst, a subject matter expert on a grand scale, and is responsible for the content of the analytical product. A typical SIO approves all finished intelligence products, coordinates budget to contract external studies, and is the unit's chief training officer. Analysts tend to be subject matter experts and are accustomed to using technology to support analysis. Liaison officers connect the analysis office either to operational forces in the field or to other organizations in the Intelligence Community. The administration/technical support staff provide a variety of functions such as disseminating the finished intelligence product, providing graphic support, and arranging travel.

Consumer Groups

Analysts produce intelligence for a number of different consumer groups.[2] These consumer groups include: (1) civilian and military policymakers; (2) military planners and executors; (3) acquisition personnel responsible for force modernization; (4) diplomatic operators; and (5) intelligence operators. Consumer groups specific to DIA analysts include (1) DIA leadership such as the Director, DIA, and the Director of Intelligence (DI); (2) Pentagon senior leadership such as Generals on the Joint Staff, other Generals in the Pentagon, and senior civilians; and (3) senior leadership in the field such as the Combatant Commanders.

Participants

This intelligence analysis benchmarking study is the result of a class project for the Joint Military Intelligence College's graduate-level course ANA 635, "Structured Techniques for Intelligence Analysts." This course helps students understand and apply descriptive and quantitative methodologies to intelligence analysis. Students were from the U.S. Air Force, U.S. Army, U.S. Navy, National Reconnaissance Office, National Imagery and Mapping Agency, and Defense Intelligence Agency. The study team worked

---

[2] A useful distinction may be drawn between "consumers" and "customers" of intelligence. Customers are those who must "pay" for the intelligence service by providing liaison officers or participating in the intelligence process in a way that drains away part of their own organization's resources. Consumers are those who are entitled to receive either standard or tailored analytic products, including briefings, but who do not find it necessary to obligate any of their own resources to its production. DIA offices typically do not recognize this distinction, and individual analysts are known to scoff at the notion that anyone for whom they provide an analytic product is a "customer" because of a perception that those who use a product are "professionals" in a sense that transcends the representation of value in dollar terms.

with five analytic units within DIA that have demonstrated excellence. The SIOs and others who met with the research team had a combined total of over 100 years of experience in intelligence analysis or related areas.

Process

The team followed established benchmarking procedures in conducting this study, which included on-site visits and interviews with members of each unit. The study team adopted a "systems" perspective that isolated the concepts of leadership, strategic planning, consumer focus, information and analysis, people and resources, process management, and mission accomplishment. Taken together, these seven elements define an organization (or a unit within a larger organization), its operations, and its performance. The information and analysis category is especially critical to the effective management of an information organization like DIA.

Exemplary Intelligence Offices

Based on their experiences, members of the JMIC faculty recommended a number of offices in the Defense Intelligence Agency as suitable interview venues for this project. The students in a structured analytic techniques class chose a subset of the organizations based on their interest in the organization. The class size limited the number of organizations that could be included in the study. Also, once officials became aware of the project and the nature of the information required, certain offices deselected themselves from the project based on their estimated lack of ability to contribute in a meaningful way. Other organizations were not available to meet with us during our limited schedule, the last few weeks of the spring quarter.

The study team visited a total number of five analysis-related organizations. Three of the organizations reside in the Directorate for Intelligence (DI). The J-2 representative who was interviewed was from a fairly small office within a much larger J-2 analysis office. He had experience in other DIA analysis offices. The JMIC respondent represented a relatively small number of faculty members with past analysis experience. Of the three DI offices, the TWC is a relatively large analysis office. The OICC, on the other hand, is a relatively small analysis-related shop that draws from the analysts within the DI to meet its mission requirements in a crisis situation. Like the OICC, the OSJ-2 is a relatively small analysis shop.

1. **Directorate for Intelligence (J2):** JCS/J-2 provides indications and warning, crisis and current intelligence support to the Office of the Secretary of Defense (OSD), the Chairman of the Joint Chiefs of Staff (JCS), Joint Staff offices, and to the Unified Commands. The J2 represents intelligence requirements of the Unified Commands, writes joint intelligence doctrine, and directs intelligence, surveillance, and reconnaissance-based assessments for the Joint Requirements Oversight Council, and the Joint Staff Director-led Joint Warfighter Capabilities Assessment teams that perform detailed assessments of programmatic alternatives, tradeoffs, risks, and effectiveness.

2. **Joint Military Intelligence College (JMIC):** The College educates military and civilian intelligence professionals and conducts and disseminates intelligence-related research.

Directorate for Intelligence Production (DI): This division manages the production of military intelligence throughout the General Defense Intelligence Program. Its products respond to intelligence needs of the OSD, JCS, Unified Commands, military services, and other U.S. government agencies. Specifically, offices for which information is developed here are:

3. **Office for Counterterrorism Analysis (TWC):** Supports the Transnational Warfare Group's efforts to detect, characterize, and assess vulnerabilities of adversary capabilities for emergent counterterrorism opportunities. TWC manages and produces all-source-intelligence in support of warfighter, policy, and acquisition communities.

4. **Operational Intelligence Coordination Center (OICC):** Exists as the focal point for crisis and contingency intelligence production within the DI. In this capacity, the OICC operates around the clock and supports the timely production and dissemination of all-source intelligence for DIA's strategic, operational, and tactical-level consumers. This effort includes the management of all intelligence taskings, requests for information, and personnel augmentation requests.

5. **Operational Environment Analysis Division (OSJ-2):** Initiates, oversees, and coordinates all-source military geographic (terrain, cultural and demographic) intelligence analysis and production required to support crisis, operational, and contingency planning efforts of the National Command Authorities (Secretaries of Defense and State), the JCS, Unified Commands, and deployed forces.

THE EVALUATION CRITERIA

The Malcolm Baldrige National Quality Improvement Act of 1987, Public Law 100-107, provides for the establishment and conduct of a national quality improvement program under which awards are given to organizations that practice effective quality management. The Act established the Malcolm Baldrige National Quality Award. In implementing this Act, the National Institute of Standards and Technology makes available guidelines and criteria designed for use by business, education and health care organizations for self-evaluation and improvement of their competitive positions.[3]   In   this paper, the NIST criteria are applied to DIA, under the premise that a U.S. government organization, through its component offices, could benefit from a systematic evaluation of its "competitive" position; namely, its ability to develop and maintain agility in a change-intensive environment.

---

[3] For background information, please see the website at URL: http://www.quality.nist.gov/.

LEADERSHIP

Leaders influence others to accomplish a mission by providing purpose, direction, and motivation. Baldrige leadership criteria apply to how the analysis organization's leader assigns tasks, interacts with analysts, and provides feedback. Within these three aspects of leader-analyst relationship, there appears to be a tension between initiative on the part of the analyst and direction on the part of the leader.

Task Assignment

Initiative. In many offices, analysis is self-generated. The office leader assigns each analyst to an area of the world and constantly pushes for finished products. The analyst is expected to act on his own initiative, do the analysis, and produce articles. In this scheme, there really is no clear top-down tasking process. One subject observed that leaders need to do a better job of prioritizing analysts' work because, even as analysts assemble data to put in databases, create briefings and produce finished intelligence products, they often write on relatively insignificant items. Their workload is usually events-driven. Consumers call in to their office and request certain information. The analysts attempt to tell the consumer what they don't already know. Their work may not always reflect the consumer's interests. To counter this tendency, some subjects maintain, managers need to incorporate a perspective on vital national interests into their analysts' tasks.

Another subject identified two ways in which analysis tasks are self-generated. In one, the analyst submits a formal proposal to do general research and, if approved, then does the work. In the second, the analyst submits a more structured proposal to study a region of the world by looking forward perhaps about 10 years. If approved, the analyst in this case identifies problems, examines them, and synthesizes them into most important issues. A problem and its attendant issues could become the basis for a National Intelligence Estimate (NIE).[4]

One subject noted that in a crisis situation, the analyst who answers the phone gets the job. For example, if the phone call comes at 1600 hours on Friday, then the analyst who has answered the phone would work with the consumer through the weekend if necessary. The study team thought that it might be difficult getting an individual to answer the phone on Friday afternoon. The subject, however, assured us that that was not the case. Indicative of the personal sense of responsibility and initiative felt by analysts, he asserted that they would actually want to get the phone call regardless of the time.

The self-generated analysis may have certain implications. First, the analysts may be doing analysis that serves the personal interest of the analyst, but does not meet a military leader's or other policymaker's requirements. Second, the analyst may be focusing atten-

---

[4] It is not uncommon for one of the National Intelligence Officers, who are the senior Intelligence Community experts on discrete topics, and who coordinate the production of NIEs, to visit with an individual analyst, or with small groups of analysts, to discuss such problems and issues.

tion on analysis projects that are the easiest or quickest to publish, satisfying a need of the analysis office, rather than producing analysis that is most beneficial to the Intelligence Community. Third, the analyst may focus on easier problems that reside in the short-term instead of tougher future-oriented problems in order to give the appearance of being more productive by producing more intelligence.

Directive. Each office leader tends to have a different method for assigning analysis tasks. In one office, the division chief ultimately assigns all tasks, regardless of the way the request comes into the subordinate office. Tasks come into an office through a "world-wide" collection management system, through internal DIA processes, through informal telephone calls from consumers, and through person-to-person memoranda. This practice may at times introduce some confusion in the office. For example, the leader may have a problem deciding whom to task. It may be appropriate to task the in-house analyst working in that area of the world, a member of a crisis response team, or a terrorist analyst.

There are certain implications when a leader directs an analyst to work a certain issue or problem. First, the leader may not be able to assign the "best" analyst because of workload. The best analyst may simply have too many projects on his or her plate or may have some other reason for making himself or herself unavailable. Second, the leader may assign a project to the wrong individual. The leader may not know who the right analyst is for a certain type of problem or issue. Third, the leader, by being too directive, may stifle the analysts' own creativity or initiative by keeping the analyst too busy.

Leader and Analyst Interaction

Initiative. Most interview subjects agreed that leaders from inside or outside their office do not interfere with the analyst's work. They provide oversight only when the analyst asks for it because analysts do not like to be micro-managed. Each manager considers his or her analysts subject matter experts. They may ask the analyst, "are you finished yet?" or "do you need help on A/B/C?" For additional support, analysts often appeal to other experts as needed.

The SIO for an office gets involved only if an analyst brings an issue or question to him. Sometimes, the SIO walks around the office, talks to the analysts, and looks for ways to help obtain certain information. The SIO gets formally involved in the analytic process, however, when the analyst has created the final product. Usually, it has been coordinated through the analyst's peers before it gets to the SIO. The SIO makes any substantive reformatting corrections before the final product can leave the office.

Directive. Usually during a crisis situation, there is face-to-face interaction between an office leader and analysts from the moment the requirement appears until it is met. One subject agreed that there should be a constant exchange of information between the leader and the analyst even during routine analysis. Some leaders are better at it than others. The lower level managers in their office worked directly with the analysts. Usually, they assign an analyst a project, discuss with them how to do it, and continually ask them how they are doing. Another subject described the production process this way: the analyst produces, the boss does a sanity-check review; the analyst coordinates his or her work with other staffs, and they suggest changes.

Feedback

Initiative. The interaction between leadership and the analyst during feedback sessions varies from office to office. It usually follows a similar pattern: the analyst produces his or her findings, managers review the work; analysts make the recommended changes, and analysts coordinate the work with appropriate offices. In some cases, the analyst decides who should coordinate on his or her analysis. Competition between offices impedes the coordination process. One subject regrets that neither top-down guidance nor tools exist to support the coordination process.

One subject said all input from leaders and peers comes after the analysis is done. As a result, the usual case is for the assessment in the final product to be conceptually close to the analyst's own findings. Once the feedback process concludes, analysts are free to post their finished products on the electronic "broadcast" media. It is usually the case that one person from an office will post products on Intelink.[5] One office included in this study posts approximately 100 products per year on Intelink. An analyst may also send a copy directly to the consumer, or may inform specific consumers of its URL. As feasible, the product will be "downgraded" to a lower classification level by obscuring sources or methods to enable it to reach a wider audience on different electronic systems.

In one office, analysts put together products on an ad hoc basis to answer requirements from consumers. Finished products are normally briefings with supplemental documents—like maps or targeting materials—published either on the shop's website or forwarded to the consumer by email or hard copy. Another method of answering a requirement is to post the answer back into the production requirements system. In one office, leaders do not actively provide formal feedback to the analyst who puts the package together. Informally, however, the shop's leader will likely be tracking the progress the analyst is making in completing the tasking by checking the finished product before it is published in any format.

Directive. After completing the analysis, the analyst will normally present his or her information to a team chief or SIO for coordination. After considering the revisions, the SIO will give the analyst permission to send written findings forward. Because this information may appear unaltered in the U.S. President's read book, an SIO does not hesitate to "wordsmith. This feedback may be frustrating and humiliating for the analyst. The SIO may direct the analyst to fix the logical development of an argument or to present more and better data. Some analysts will simply rework their product and resubmit it to the SIO. Others, however, will discuss the comments with the SIO. The SIO typically prefers the latter method because the analyst will usually understand the comments better and

---

[5] Intelink is the Community's intranet, hosting "value-added" intelligence products.

will learn more from the experience. Almost all of the products go to their consumers; only rarely will a product be killed within the analyst's office.

Leaders tend to squelch any negative commentary on U.S. information operations (IO) issues. Their attitudes reflect an Intelligence Community-wide aversion to discussing IO problems associated with the U.S. or "blue" force. Intelligence analysts are free to discuss "red" force issues, but only military operations officers or "operators" are free to discuss "blue" force issues. As a result, decisionmakers must learn to seek information about the "blue" force from one source and information about the "red" force from another. They must combine the information themselves in order to get a full picture of the situation.

One subject suggested that ideally the analyst can encourage short, regular feedback sessions from the manager on an informal basis. For example, if the boss wanted a briefing for a future meeting, the analyst could give him some draft charts well ahead of time and expect nearly immediate feedback. In practice, however, the boss often edits only the final charts and returns them to the analyst who is forced under pressure of time to make the necessary changes. Interview subjects frequently alluded to this problem, and opine that such feedback issues remain a problem. Interview subjects nevertheless offered the following examples of good, direct feedback. First, an individual who was quite good at making changes would eliminate unnecessary words, shortening the report and making the wording much tighter. The analysts expressed appreciation of this feedback because of the value added to the product. In the second example, a manager was very good at grooming new managers. He would receive an analyst's report, then hand it to another analyst to review and comment. In this way, subjects noted, he was developing new leaders.

Comments

Good leadership demands high quality products to inform warfighters and policymakers. Leaders need analysis to answer tough questions. At the same time, managers need to keep in mind important questions about the analysis process itself:

- Are military leaders able to do their job better because of their analyst's product?

- Are the benefits of doing the analysis outweighing the costs?

- Are we doing risk analysis? That is, are we attempting to understand the balance between threat and vulnerabilities by examining local trade-offs?

Good leadership ensures a value-added coordination process. Analysts often find the coordination process tough. One subject said that before the first draft, the analyst's job was the best job. After the first draft, however, the analyst's job was difficult. Another subject called into question the coordination process because of the low quality of finished products posted in the database. Another subject said the coordination process is a humbling experience for the analyst because it is tough to get back your paper marked up with corrections. One subject said a co-worker tested the system. He worked really hard on one project and sent it forward. Next time, he slapped something together and sent it forward.

He noticed that it didn't make any difference either way. He was devastated. There was no motivation to excel. From these testimonials, one could conclude that unsystematized (non-standard) coordination may hinder the work of analysts.

Good leadership theoretically removes such barriers to effective use of analytical resources by providing leading-edge administrative and computer support; quick-turn-around graphics support for urgent tasks; and hassle-free travel support. One subject compared DIA administrative support unfavorably with what he grew to expect when he worked for the Central Intelligence Agency. He could drop something off at 5PM for graphics support and pick it up when he got to work in the morning. When he traveled, his proactive travel office would remove some of the hassles associated with traveling. He would tell someone in the travel office where he needed to go. They would call him back a short time later with all the information he needed to know about the trip. Then, when he got back from his trip, he told them what he did and they reimbursed him. There were no required travel reports and no receipts. In fact, they told him to get rid of all his receipts. In case he was caught; it would be better for no one else to know where he had been! One reason the DIA may be different is the fact that the CIA focuses more on covert operations than the DIA. Another reason is that DIA, a DoD organization, has stricter accountability rules and regulations than the CIA. As a result, the DIA analysts must do a better job of documenting their trip for accountability purposes. It would probably not be possible for the DIA to adopt the CIA process without some changes in the laws that govern travel accountability.

Good leadership intervenes to handle sensitive, political aspects of a job. Leaders may be able to supply the needed leverage or "muscle." For example, a limited number of analysts may be qualified to handle issues in a crisis situation. A trade-off may need to be negotiated between support for the warfighter and support for senior policymakers in the Pentagon, all within the Department of Defense. Further, leaders may need to intervene to facilitate interaction between the analyst and consumers in order to ensure that analysts anticipate and meet their consumers' priorities.

Summary

Leadership is a critical aspect in determining the success of the intelligence analysis process. Leadership demands high-quality products, ensures a value-added coordination process, removes technical or administrative barriers, and intervenes when needed. Some leaders assign tasks directly to the analysts. Others rely on the Senior Intelligence Officer (SIO) to assign tasks or rely on the initiative of the analysts themselves to seek out the right problems and analyze them. Leadership tends to provide little or no interaction during the analysis process except if and when the analyst seeks it. Analysts do not like to be micro-managed. In a crisis situation however, the leader takes a more direct and hands-on approach. Although feedback varied from office to office, ideally the analyst should seek short, regular feedback on an informal basis with the office leader.

STRATEGIC PLANNING

Baldrige criteria compel an examination of how an analysis office prepares for future challenges, records its institutional history, and uses academic or professional sources. Within the category of future challenges, a distinction may be made between *capability* and *issue* challenges. Future *capability* challenges deal with the people and process issues. Future *issue* challenges, on the other hand, are country- or target-dependent. These challenges deal specifically with the emerging threat to U.S. interests. Although none of the offices has a written, formal strategic plan, in most, leaders claimed to have thought about strategic planning issues and were working toward a future vision. Their daily mission though was to "get the right information to the right people at the right time."

Future Challenges

Capability Challenges. Organizational capability centers on people and processes. For those subjects who indicated that they have thought about the future in strategic planning terms, leaders recognized that the commitment of their people to an organizational ideal is a necessary ingredient for success. In practice, then, organizational capabilities must support strategic planning. Analysis organizations need to consider their staff capabilities and ensure that staffs have the necessary knowledge, skills, and tools for success. Our study subjects generally favored a team approach for intelligence analysis. Leaders wanted analysts to consult with experts and coordinate with stakeholders before sending the final product to consumers.

Most office representatives said they had just the right mix of people for their mission. In one instance, an office had been given an abundance of people and other resources. However, if some other offices only had a few more people or more resources, then they too would be able to do much more for their consumers. Since they were already meeting their mission requirements, they did not expect to have additional people bestowed on them. In fact, office leaders reported that they had to fight annually to maintain their personnel resources, as many capabilities are fungible from one office to another. One office among those examined expected to hire several more entry-level people. An advantage of this approach is that new people tend to be more computer-literate than older staff members. An unsurprising tradeoff is that new people also tend to be less well-educated, in a professional sense, in their specialty. Another subject said there was no real future planning for their office personnel. The objective was to get analysts through identified training requirements so they could produce reports in order to fill databases.

Since none of the subjects claimed to use a formal strategic planning process, our study team could not discuss the process with them in detail. A generic strategic planning process, however, should include (1) doing advanced planning, (2) performing an environmental scan based on external and internal information, (3) setting a strategic direction using the vision statement, (4) translating the strategic direction into action via an implementation plan, and (5) making a performance evaluation. A performance evaluation or assessment should include (1) defining goals, (2) describing success, (3) setting targets, (4) measuring performance, and (5) adjusting goals based on performance. The DIA has a formal process to do strategic planning, but it was not clear to the study team how the organizational strategic planning process might be linked to the lower levels of the organization.

Issue Challenges. Concern about issues centers on the mission of each analysis office. Evidence from this study indicates that an SIO often thinks about future issues. For example, he may hire external contractors to investigate an area of interest. One office recently commissioned a study to look out 5-10 years and make recommendations on a specific issue. Those recommendations addressed the question of what they needed to do now in order to prepare themselves for the envisioned future. One subject stressed the extant ability of his office to remain flexible and to evolve thoughtfully, guided by its own resources and instincts. As evidence in support of such confidence, he noted the office's demonstrated ability to anticipate warfighter needs. Another subject asserted that his office simply follows issues (in the widest "all-source" sense) as they are developing so when they are called to support a requirement, they are aware of what is going on and may have some work completed already.

One subject offered an example of an office in CIA that he was invited to join a few years ago. It was a new organization and analysts joined it by invitation only. Analysts regarded it as a fun place to work because they had an opportunity to be innovative. The office wanted to look at the world in a new way. One type of project associated with this office was a study of demographic changes and political instability within the major cities of a certain foreign country. He said they wrote five case study documents covering these places of interest in considerable detail. Such detail on individual cities was unusual for an Intelligence Community product, and at the same time greatly appreciated by consumers. According to our subject, this office no longer exists in the CIA. When offering it as an example of good intelligence, he implied that it may be worthwhile for DIA to stand up an office like the former CIA office to deal with today's complex issues.

Institutional History

Most subjects said they did not have a written institutional history. There exist no formal analyses of their office's strengths or weaknesses. The office does rely, then, on retaining experienced individuals for its corporate memory.[6] Some offices maintain briefings about their office's operations as a surrogate for a written institutional history. Anyone assigned to an analytic unit is expected to set about building connections and learning operations and systems. Only one subject said they had formed a history office to record significant events for their office, beginning in the late 1990s. Even this admirable initiative, however, with its focus on events, rather that process itself, would fail to capture the nuances of truly useful and recoverable institutional history.[7]

Academic or Professional Sources

In the interviews, office leaders tended to support academic training, attendance at professional conferences and conventions as experiences useful to the development of professional expertise. However, there exist at the office level no guides or plans for such professionalization opportunities.[8] Within an office, professionalization appears to be driven from the bottom up. If an analyst learns about a class or other certifiable learning opportunity, the agency's training center resources can assist with financial support, assuming office politics and workload do not intervene. Interviews revealed that little

---

[6] DIA does operate a mentoring program to ensure that some corporate memory is passed to younger analysts. Facilitated mentoring can cut on-the-job training time by up to half and may be a key factor in the retention of entry-level hires. However, participation in the mentoring program is relatively small compared to the entire workforce. Even if some employees enter into a mentoring relationship, there is no guarantee that the process will be successful. Potential pitfalls include: unrealistic expectations, supervisor unsupportive, relationship derails, shortage of good mentors, differences (style, ethnicity, gender, age) interfere, and relationship is a poor fit. Although U.S. Government and Department of Defense regulations do require that agency, and by extension, office products and communications be preserved as official records, the combined procedural and target knowledge required to create actionable intelligence typically escapes being recorded in the impersonal domain of such records.

[7] One exception to this rule is the Agency's *Military and Geographic Intelligence Cookbook*. The Joint Military Intelligence College also offers an exception to this state of affairs, with its publications *Writing with Intelligence* (August 1995), *Briefing with Intelligence* (August 1997) and *Research: Design and Methods* (September 2000), which capture the combined experience of student and faculty interaction in teaching and learning about intelligence studies.

[8] Career development is a continuous career-long process of self-assessment and planning that helps employees integrate their career goals with their organization's mission and needs. The DIA Career Development System (CDS) is designed to assist employees in career planning and development. Components of the CDS include: entry level development program, designed to train and develop entry-level employees, and the career service program, designed to enhance DIA's work environment and improve employee productivity.

emphasis is likely to emanate from office or division managers. Most requests are driven by personal interest and are authorized so long as funds exist to support it.

Each analysis office uses academic and professional sources in a different way. One office hires contractors to provide them with computer support. Another office employs over 100 contractors and academics to perform tasks in an external research program. In this case, according to interview testimony, analysts are able to integrate the outside research into their daily operations only with some difficulty. For example, analysts in this unit had to learn how to integrate data on cyber-terrorism and IO into counterterrorism analysis. Representatives from one office visited Unified Command Joint Intelligence Centers to learn to do this better. Another office used the *Military and Geographic Intelligence Cookbook* (MAGIC) to inform their analysts of "everything they needed to know to do their job." If the analysts had not used a specific tool in a while, then they consulted MAGIC to refresh their memory.

Richards J. Heuer, Jr., a senior CIA analyst, has tried to acquaint analysts at that agency with methodological developments in socio-political analysis that were being developed and tested in the academic world. He had to keep at it for more than a decade to be heard.[9] He has often met with strong resistance. Only a few academics willingly come to the agency to talk with the analysts. "Factions," an analytical tool developed at CIA for systematic analysis of political instability, is a good example of research and development (R&D) work done in collaboration with members of the academic community.[10] In the 1980s there was no particular pressure or encouragement across the Community to use structured analytic methods. Analysts gathered the facts, looked at them in their uniquely "logical" way, and came to some conclusions. Some DIA analysts use structured techniques to do intelligence analysis. The subjects we spoke to, however, described their analytical process as gathering facts, examining them logically and drawing some conclusions. More emphasis on structured techniques at DIA may be appropriate.

Summary

Although none of our subjects had a written, formal strategic plan, most of them had thought about strategic planning issues and were working toward a future common vision

---

[9] Finally, on 20 June 2000, at the inauguration of CIA's Sherman Kent School, which features a curriculum for new analysts, Heuer's campaign reached a pinnacle of acceptance by the agency, evidenced by his book's, *Psychology of Intelligence Analysis* (Washington, DC: Center for the Study of Intelligence, 1999), being the focus of remarks by invited speakers. Another senior CIA analyst, Morgan Jones, had a few years earlier published a compact summary of "Fourteen Powerful Techniques for Problem Solving," some of them having been developed exclusively by agency analysts, in *The Thinker's Toolkit* (New York: Random House, Times Books, 1995), reprinted in a slightly revised edition in 1998 by Random House's Times Business division..

[10] Stanley A. Feder, "Factions and Policon: New Ways to Analyze Politics," reprinted from CIA's *Studies in Intelligence in* H. Bradford Westerfield's *Inside CIA's Private World* (New Haven, CT: Yale University Press, 1995), 274-292.

among the personnel in their office. Office leadership is often engaged with senior leadership about future issues. Managers know the direction they want to go in and recognize the need to support a strategic plan. Furthermore, a focus on important future issues such as which country is most problematic clearly makes an analysis shop proactive and saves time in crisis situations.

Theoretically, the strategic management process includes (1) advanced planning; (2) an environmental scan that includes a review of internal and external information; (3) setting a strategic direction; (4) translating the strategic direction into action; and (5) evaluating performance. Consumers, stakeholders, and subjects influence the process by stating their requirements, receiving products and services, and providing feedback. Information and analysis influence each step of the process by providing management with important information, data, and feedback.

Most of our subjects relied on the corporate memory of senior analysts instead of maintaining a recorded institutional history. As senior analysts approach retirement age and leave government service, analysis offices will lose a great deal of expertise. Some offices maintained a written office history or had on file significant briefings about their office's operations. All of our subjects used academic or professional sources to develop their capabilities as needed. They also knew what commercial tools were available to help them to do more for their consumers.

CONSUMER FOCUS

The Baldrige criteria applicable to a consumer focus suit the DIA case very well. As an information organization, this agency is obligated, through its analysis units, to discern consumers' requirements. A key question for this study is whether relationships with consumers tend to be *ad hoc* or the result of a deliberate strategy.

Consumer Requirements

Consumers make their requirements known through a formal production database, telephone calls, individual initiatives, by e-mail, and through personal visits. They make their initial requirements known primarily on an *ad hoc* basis. The most meaningful requirements are informal because the analyst gets to talk directly to the consumer. Subsequently, the analyst can help the consumer refine the formal request in the Community's intelligence production database. Some consumers make telephone calls to analysts that require an answer in two hours or less. This can make the analyst's job very stressful. Consumers use emails, on the other hand, as a secondary contact medium and mostly for follow-up activities. On occasion, a consumer will come to the analyst's office to maximize the opportunity to gain a very specific pre-deployment, contextual understanding of target information. One subject noted that although most analytic tasks are management-driven, there are also many self-generated products. The latter could have a positive effect, especially in promoting analyst self-esteem, so long as the self-generated products are of interest to the entire Community. In one case made known to the study team, an office leader asked analysts simply to produce products for their databases. As a result, analysts chose subjects that they could write about more easily in order to meet their deadlines, rather than picking topics that represent the "tough questions" and that would be most useful to the Community in general.

Consumer and Analyst Interaction

The different frames of reference that one might expect to characterize any interaction between analysts and consumers are on vivid display in anecdotes related by most interview subjects. Much of the time, consumers appear to shy away from direct interaction with an analyst. On occasion, the consumer's rank is too far above that of the analyst to allow an analyst to directly approach an individual consumer, especially in an organization like DIA, often still characterized by a culture that finds meaning in and derives behavioral clues from a hierarchy of authority. Occasionally, however, informal interaction does occur, to include face-to-face conversations or telephone calls to enhance clarity of requirements. One subject noted that his contact with consumers is mainly personal and direct. This analyst works with consumers to build training products that look as much as possible like the real world. Toward that end, an analyst might attend survival school as a student, rather than as a VIP, in order to absorb and then re-create more realistically some part of that training environment. On issues related to training, analysts tend to go to wherever their consumers are located. There, they interact directly and build products together. Consumers also come to DIA. For example, one analyst recounted his experience with a Navy SEAL who sat next to the analyst during the production process. In another example, one analyst worked closely with an Air Force consumer on a downed pilot evacuation and recovery area study.

Some subjects claimed to have little or no interaction with consumers. One subject said there was some consumer support at the analyst-to-analyst level and through informal channels. As a general rule, however, there is no regular contact with a consumer. Therefore, the role of consumer often is represented by whoever becomes a reader of a particular publication.[11] Production tasking usually passes through bureaucratic levels at both the producer and consumer ends, which reinforces pre-existing tendencies keeping analysts and consumers away from each other. Suddenly, an answer to a formal or informal request simply appears. A general absence of feedback from consumers characterizes the intelligence production process in the offices included in this study. Any interaction with consumers that does occur happens on an *ad hoc* basis.

---

[11] Because most products are published electronically on systems such as Intelink, it is possible for the agency to track in considerable detail the organizations and even particular analysts that access and explore particular documents. In practice, however, this is rarely done at the level of detail that allows an analyst to be certain who the consumer really may be. Even if one accepts the concept that within the Department of Defense, information becomes actionable intelligence mainly through the briefing process, it is wise to remember that cognitive processes do depend ultimately on purposeful information-seeking activity, which can hypothetically be tracked in such detail as to inform intelligence producers exactly who their true consumers really are.

Feedback

Analysts provide finished products to their consumers in a variety of ways: through the formal production requirements management database, in hard copy, posted to a website, or by email. Sometimes, depending on the size of the electronic file, analysts post a product on a "hidden" URL. Then, they call a known consumer to let them know where they have posted the product. Once the consumer has the product, the analyst can delete it from the system. Feedback appears in many forms. In one office, informal feedback predominates through personal contact with the consumers. Another office obtains consumer feedback either via the office web site's "feedback" button, or via a verbal response from the consumer that the product met or did not meet the need. Hard copies automatically include a publication office's formal feedback form. All products do not get this form. One subject said a team in their division uses a questionnaire to find out if their consumers liked their product. One office maintains a sizable travel budget so analysts may travel to their consumer's office regularly.

Sometimes analysts are told when they did a good job. They are also told when they could have done better, a phenomenon that has become more common with the advent of impersonal electronic communication. Consumers can be very specific. Analysts provide briefings to their consumers and they attend briefings by consumers. They may get a phone call saying either "great job," or that the Admiral wants to know why the analyst came to a certain conclusion. Sometimes, the analyst writes for a specific individual. The individual consumer almost always responds positively in this scenario. If the product goes directly from the analytic office to an individual, then there are not many levels of review. In such a case, reviewers will include a (1) branch chief, (2) the DIA Office of Research, and (3) the Division Chief. If, however, the analysis office broadcasts the product, then the review process can reach extremes of review and coordination.

Marketing a product can attain great importance. An analyst typically does not want his or her finished product to sit on the table in the J-2's office. The usual desire is for the information to reach much lower levels, where the material remains actionable information, which may only later become actionable *intelligence*. They do this by using different means of communication. For example, they publish their results using different media such as in the *Military Intelligence Digest*, which features strategic or operational assessments; the general finished intelligence database, known as Intelink; serialized DIA publications, and informal contacts with consumers around the world. The analyst who writes the product can market it by mailing hard copies, by telling people where to find it on Intelink or by responding to specific requests by sending email attachments or making a personal phone call.

Summary

Building relationships with consumers tends to be more *ad hoc* than the result of a deliberate strategy. Although consumer feedback varies from office to office, most of the subjects said that "working-level" consumers support their intelligence analysis process. Some got feedback from an office web site. Others got it through verbal interaction. If funding is available, then analysts visit their consumers often to learn about their requirements and get feedback about past performance. Often these consumers will visit the shop to let them know what they need and to describe how particular, related products have been used in similar situations in the past.

Likewise, the way consumers make their requirements known varies from office to office. Consumers continuously provide information as they themselves move along in the analysis process.[12] Analysts preferred a phone call from the consumer first so they could coach the consumer through the process of documenting their needs in the COLISEUM database. Once the analyst completes the product, they market their work. Analysts used different methods to make their products available, improve their chances of getting their information to the appropriate consumers, and ensure consumers have an opportunity to use their product.

INFORMATION AND ANALYSIS

Information and analysis criteria address the question of how well DIA offices are meeting challenges in this core functional area, and reveal whether a meaningful approach is being taken by the organization for measuring product quality. Representatives of most of the analysis offices indicated that they are meeting the requirements embodied in these criteria. Informal means for measuring analysis performance included counting products, meeting production schedules, regularly updating databases, answering key consumer-oriented questions, and gauging performance based on "perception."

Meeting Current Analytic Challenges

Specific indicators of success that were quickly asserted by interview subjects included the following:

1. Positive comments or lack of negative comments from consumers;
2. Evidence of consumer use of intelligence products;
3. Knowledge of the number of terrorist attacks averted;
4. A downward trend in the number of requests for information (RFI);
5. Evidence of improvement of analysts' capabilities based on accumulated experience.

---

[12] DIA has begun serious promotion of collaborative intelligence production across the defense intelligence agencies, military service intelligence production facilities and among Unified Command Joint Intelligence Centers through the Joint Intelligence Virtual Architecture Program (JIVA). This program allows individual analysts from across the defense intelligence community to rapidly find, access, and use trusted information of all types and classification, without knowing its location or format, and to do their jobs easier, faster and better. JIVA provides a virtual, interactive environment for the development and exchange of responsive, tailored all-source Intelligence and value-added analysis.

Subjects easily enumerated evidence associated with each of these indicators. For example, if consumers are satisfied with the analyst's work, then they provide positive feedback via any number of methods. The amount of positive feedback, however, is usually meager. Not surprisingly, a tendency exists for a dissatisfied consumer to be more vocal. A lack of negative comments from consumers is therefore considered a positive indicator of success. Consumers never want DIA to stop sending them daily intelligence products. Even if routine DIA assessments are only placeholders, the consumer still expresses a demand for the products because one article could change everything.

Whether the consumer uses the intelligence product is another indicator of success. Analysts do need to know how many consumers read DIA products and find them useful. In actuality, a production office is only rarely able to gauge the use and impact of either particular products, or the office's overall production. Ideally, the office's products are suited for use without modification, as formal or informal coordination is expected to contribute meaningfully to the production of each item. The concept of usability depends on being able to measure whether information embodied in the office's products are "actionable." Measurement of actionability is never easy because often no recordable action is required, and the producer faces the difficult task of determining whether the product has simply influenced the way a consumer views an important issue. No one from among the offices under study here claims to have an answer to this difficult issue.

Likewise, a great indicator of success would be the number of terrorist attacks averted. It is rare, however, for DIA to learn about a terrorist cell whose members talk about an act of terrorism, prepare the attack, and then stop as a result of DIA's informing the specific target or the larger public. With continued capabilities to collect information without the target's knowledge, measurement of such occurrences is certainly feasible. With increased emphasis on collaborative counterterrorism analysis, some of the best minds in the Intelligence Community are now addressing this very problem.

DIA analysts often find themselves responding to formal Requests for Information (RFIs) from consumers. Another positive measurement standard, then, although an indirect one with the potential for unknown intervening variables, is a downward trend in the number of RFIs. Analysts do assume they are doing something right if the number of RFIs from active consumers are declining in number. Of course, if only a few RFIs make up this measurement, then some means of weighting the breadth of the requests needs to be considered. Over the course of a year, however, the substantial number of RFIs would allow the laws of probability to operate in support of attaching meaning to a statistically significant decline in overall RFI numbers. Nevertheless, at least among the offices in this study, no such statistically based measurement is practiced.

A different type of indicator of success is the level of improvement in analyst savvy, given the accumulation of experience. An office's SIO is in a good position to determine whether the analyst is making improvement. Comments from the SIOs contacted in the course of this study indicate that they examine the analyst's work with a critical eye to determine whether the analyst is growing in the job. If it is determined that the analyst is in fact getting better at doing analysis, then the SIO rewards the analyst with more work and more challenging jobs. The SIO also rewards the analysts with an appropriate performance review. If however, the analyst does not show improvement in the current task, then the SIO working with the analyst and manager will attempt to diagnose the problem and provide appropriate training to improve proficiency in doing analysis.

One indicator of success that is not appropriate is that associated with a specific forecast of events. One subject noted that one must be cautious in making such a forecast, and then watching to see if the projection is correct. Office representatives observe that this approach does not constitute a good indicator of success because it may be misleading to track, as analysts have the opportunity to continually reshape their forecasts and analysts and professionals do not like the idea of being graded on their own judgment calls. To illustrate, one time an analyst wrote a paper on Kenya. The prediction was that Kenya would be stable over the next five years. In the third year, however, a destabilizing coup was attempted. The analyst had failed to account for a coup attempt, but since the coup failed, the analyst's judgment was confirmed—he was correct. But were the analyst and his product really successful?

A Standard Approach to Measuring Quality

No subject claimed to have plans to implement any kind of standard approach to measure analytic quality. One subject said he was not opposed to some standard for measuring quality. He has not, however, seen a useful measure for it. In another office, analysts "just publish in order to keep their database filled." Little or no attention is given to quality. Either the product meets the requirement or it doesn't. Another subject said even if he thought measuring analytic quality was a good idea, no one in his office would do it. Managers in his office, however, are examining ways to do things more effectively without destroying the office's "can-do" ethos.

Comments

All of the subjects said they had no formal performance measurements, but neither did they employ informal means. To justify this situation, one subject said intelligence analysis is purely subjective. There are no numbers to count. If analysts meet their production schedule, then they are considered to be successful. If analysts get all of their work done, then they have met the minimum success requirement. If analysts get all of their work done and they are also able to get *ad hoc* work done too, then they are considered more successful. No one interviewed would accept the idea that there may exist valid quantitative measures of analytical success.

Managers of intelligence analysis are ambivalent about managing for results. Though interested in demonstrating success, they are uneasy about being held accountable for poor organizational performance. There are severe problems in measuring performance in practice: (1) problems in getting agreement on what good performance means for intelligence analysis; (2) intelligence analysis goals are unreasonable compared with available resources; (3) key performance indicators are unavailable or too costly to collect; and (4) management is unwilling to make necessary changes to improve intelligence analysis.

Informal evaluation of analytical quality of course does occur. In many cases, an office SIO is expected to contribute to an analyst's performance evaluation. For example, the SIO might show the division chief examples of the analyst's work and point out what is good about it, what is a problem or an opportunity for improvement, and whether the analyst has learned from experience. Office leaders appear to be most interested in how many products the analyst finished, even though this crude measure is not supplemented with any method for independently weighting the relative value of those products.

One subject noted that his office does track certain indicators of quality, such as whether the consumer liked the product. A subsidiary indicator lies in evidence of whether the consumer responded to the product. Did anyone else want a copy of the product? Some have developed a measure of the significance of the problems they analyze. For example, an imminent terrorism problem, compared to a future military planning problem is more significant and would fit on of the high end of their measurement scale. The SIO or division chief for this office would maintain a matrix of products by author and subject.

One subject prefers using the term "gauge" instead of "measure" because "measure" assumes some sort of reasoned technique. Often, there is a bit of a "gut check" in any office with respect to how well managers perceive their office to be meeting its mission. Most of the measurement comes in the form of *ad hoc* consumer feedback. A well-executed mission, like a successful noncombatant evacuation operation (NEO) for instance, tells the office that they are doing a good job.

Summary

Informal means for measuring analysis performance included counting products, meeting production schedule, updating databases, answering key consumer-oriented questions, and gauging performance based on perception. Two common ways for analysts to know if they are meeting their consumer's needs are by a lack of negative feedback and by an increase in product use. Our subjects do not keep track of forecast accuracy because it is too difficult to track. Instead analysts individually keep a mental checklist on any forecasts they make and how the situation developed over time. Although none of our subjects planned to implement any standard approach to measure analytic quality in the near future, they continue to examine ways to do analysis more effectively without destroying their organization's "can do" ethos.

PEOPLE AND RESOURCES

The people and resources category offers criteria to examine the knowledge, skills, and experiences of the analysts and the availability of analysts' tools. Leaders can improve the quality of a product by promoting greater expertise among the intelligence analysts and by inducing analysts to take advantage of information found in open sources. Study subjects said they need analysts who think across interdisciplinary boundaries and they prefer analysts who have military operations experience.

Most of our subjects assert that they are well-qualified to perform their mission. One office was gaining personnel resources quickly because their issue is very visible. In the recent past, the boss would train the new analysts. Today, however, the office that has grown so rapidly finds that even the bosses are all new. They appear to need a formal training program targeted at the office level, rather than merely at individuals.[13] Another office whose personnel resources were static considered itself successful because they are meeting their requirements. They could be better if they had better tools and if they had a few more people in the office. They note that static personnel resourcing makes them less successful than they could be, but not unsuccessful. Another office claimed to be under-staffed. To make matters worse, they suggest that they have the "wrong" people in management positions. Even within the small sample of offices in this study, there appeared some examples of high-interest areas where analysts whose experience had been gained in other functional areas are now "parked" pending retirement. This is clearly a poor management practice. It is the result of an archaic government personnel system and is common practice throughout government.

Knowledge, Skills, and Experience

According to representatives of the five offices in DIA, analysts bring with them or develop certain skills to help them perform their analysis and at the same time they must develop an awareness of how certain analytic pitfalls may influence their work. The analytic skills include: (1) technical or topical expertise; (2) knowledge of the target, sources, and analytic techniques; (3) ability to search and organize data; (4) ability to synthesize data or use inductive reasoning; and (5) ability to express ideas. The analytic pitfalls include: (1) personal biases or inexperience; (2) lack of data or access to data; (3) asking the wrong question;[14] (4) misunderstanding data; (5) flaws in logic; (6) no review or evaluation process; (7) denial and deception by the target; (8) politicization or non-objectivity; (9) groupthink; and (10) mirror imaging.

A synthesis of interviews conducted for this study suggests that analysts need to learn how to think across disciplinary boundaries. As a general rule, analysts do not learn to think across disciplinary boundaries in school. One subject suggested that analysts could take (remedial) philosophy courses in order to learn how to think across disciplinary boundaries. Another subject suggested that cross-disciplinary education continued in their

---

[13] Joint Military Intelligence Training Center courses are designed for students who have no experience or have limited previous experience in intelligence at the joint, combined, or national levels and have job-related requirements for knowledge of intelligence at the national or strategic levels.

[14] The problem of asking the wrong, or the right, question is especially noticeable in strategic analysis, the type of analysis produced by DIA in support of the Chairman of the JCS and the National Command Authorities. This problem has been addressed succinctly and with examples in Patrick J. Haney, "Soccer Fields and Submarines in Cuba: The Politics of Problem Definition," *Naval War College Review* 50, no. 4 (Augumn 1997): 67-84.

shop because personnel possess deep knowledge in history, political science, and economics. These people also had computer skills, and 5 to 25 years of intelligence analysis experience each. One subject added that the people in their office who started DIA employment in the 1980s had fewer computer skills, but knew more about their subject matter. Younger people tend to be gifted at using digits to display information. Their elders claim that they lack the skills necessary to infuse meaning into the displays.

One subject said they have area specialists, social scientists, former military personnel, former law enforcement agents, active-duty military professionals, and reservists with long active-duty backgrounds. They like having an office filled with people who have the different perspectives. They have senior people with lots of experience. Then there is a big drop-off in experience among the lower level staff members. One problem frequently voiced is that new hires top out in four years at the GS-13 level, then they have to move out of the office to continue advancing in their career. A consensus exists among office managers that any office struggles to maintain their analysis capability as people move to better jobs for promotion. Having people who are career intelligence officers, especially if they also possess a military operations background, is commonly cited as a key to a quality staff.

Tools

Subjects of this study reported using a variety of common tools to accomplish their missions. These tools included:

- COLISEUM (Community On-Line Intelligence System for End Users and Managers-- an intelligence production requirements database);
- JWICS (Joint Worldwide Intelligence Communications System--featuring Intelink, the Community's finished intelligence database), Websafe (a message handling system) and VTC (Video Teleconferencing) to communicate with consumers;
- SIPRNET (Secret Internet Protocol Router Network);
- OSIS (Open Source Information System), and NIPRNet (Non-classified Internet Protocol Router Network);
- DITDS (Defense Intelligence Threat Data System);
- DIA and DODIIS (DoD Intelligence Information System) e-mail.

Analysts use a variety of techniques and tools to produce intelligence. Techniques include pattern analysis, systems analysis, quantitative analysis, modeling, and inductive reasoning. Analysts use tools specific to their form of analysis. These tools include the following:

- *The Analyst's Notebook*, featuring visual investigative analysis software that assists analysts by uncovering, interpreting, and displaying complex information in easily understood chart form. It includes a link notebook for link analysis and a case notebook for time-event analysis.
- *Hugin Expert* is artificial intelligence software based on Bayesian analysis. Bayesian analysis is a compact model for representing reasoning under uncertainty.

■ *ESRI* (Environmental Systems Research Institute) GIS (Geographic Information System) is a core set of application tools for organizing and analyzing geographic information. *ArcView* includes powerful visualization tools to create maps.

Summary

Analysts need to be able to think across interdisciplinary boundaries and have military operations experience. Senior analysts tend to be subject matter experts. Newer analysts, however, tend to be more computer literate. Our subjects liked having staffs with a diverse mix of experiences. They recommended tools such as the analyst's notebook which features time-event analysis and link-analysis; *Hugin Expert* which features Bayesian network analysis; and *ESRI GIS* which contains ARC-View. They also use numerous intelligence-related classified databases and other open sources.

PROCESS MANAGEMENT

Process management criteria apply to information handling, intelligence analysis, and collaboration. Processes associated with the dissemination of information and intelligence are beyond the scope of this study, but in this area, the advent of online publication and the loosening of "need to know" rules governing access to sensitive information have relieved some classic dissemination bottlenecks.[15] Good analysts are commonly characterized by DIA officials as "focused freethinkers." Other commonly acknowledged maxims are that the analysis process is a highly competitive process, and that analysts rush to be first to publish vital intelligence findings. At the same time, analysts must work together by collaborating with other analysts to ensure accuracy.

None of our subjects said they observed a formal or structured process in doing intelligence analysis. One subject summed up this approach as simply "sitting down and going to work." A second subject claimed to use an informal and semi-structured, term research process. In this mode, the analyst first has an idea related to their "account." They discuss with their team chief the problem they are interested in solving. If they get permission, then they do the research. Another subject added that, likewise, he does not have a "hard-wired" approach, yet applies a routine to the process. One subject said his office has a process that only remains in the mind of each of the office's analysts. It is, in the estimation of this subject, an application of the scientific method or at least a disciplined thought process. In this scheme, managers give the analyst a problem, and the analyst does research to determine what they have and what they need. If there is time, he or she will request collection of certain data. The analyst reviews the data and answers the question. Sometimes, the analyst will get feedback (either good job or please do better next time). Typically across the offices examined here, there is no standardized way of conducting

---

[15]Modification of the "need to know" principle as it applies to information systems has been accompanied by the use of effective counterintelligence tools that allow detailed tracking of actions taken by individual analysts in the handling of sensitive information.

analysis. This situation may be a tacit response to the philosophy expressed by office leaders that they try to encourage "out-of-the-box" thinking.

Information Handling

Analysts do their own fieldwork to gather any information beyond that from routinely available, written sources. One SIO emphasized that his analysts "gather" information, they do not "collect" it. For example, they do not have diplomatic immunity when they are visiting other countries; they must get specific permission from the country to be there. Standard Community information is derived from imagery, signals, human resources, "open" sources, and other technical means. The kind of information that analysts use is problem-dependent. They may use operations-support products such as maps, imagery, and target materials. Some analysts tend to use information from the source with which they feel most comfortable. For example, some like using signals information and rely solely on it. Office leaders typically try to accustom analysts to using multiple sources of information including the Internet.

Analysts report that they try to lay down the steps of their analysis in a logical way. For example, they use several paths to move from general information to more specific information. Some analysts write their papers as if they were doing research in a graduate school. Others write products that look like newspaper articles. Analysts tend to protect their sources in a manner similar to the way newspaper reporters protect the identity of their sources. They use a general description to protect the identity of the informant. For example, a writer may attribute a quote to a high level authority in a specific DoD organization such as the Pentagon. The reader may judge for him or herself whether the source is reliable, but is unable to precisely identify the source.

Intelligence Analysis Process

The analysis process includes (1) problem identification; (2) data gathering; (3) analysis, synthesis, collaboration, and examination of alternative propositions using all sources of data; and (4) direct support to consumers with briefings and publications. In the end, analysts make an assessment of what the data probably mean or what the data could mean. General Colin Powell (USA, Ret.) sums up his expectations as a consumer of intelligence in this way: "Tell me what you know, what you don't know, and what you think— in that order." In this oft-quoted dictum, he suggests that analysts can best convey what is known about the problem, evaluate the completeness of their knowledge, and interpret its meaning. It remains unclear whether the same guidance is as suitable for written products as for oral briefings. In the course of analysis, whether presented in written or oral format, it is important for the analyst to answer for himself certain key questions:

1. What do you know about the issue?

2. What is a logical, sequential way to present the facts?

3. What conclusions or implications can be drawn from these facts?

Analysts generally find it distasteful to coordinate their products with members outside of their team. Nonetheless, when the "corporate" analysis process works as it can, all of the teams contribute to the analyst's final product and, as a result, the analyst produces a superior product. Managers do want analysts to exchange information with each other. They have a distaste for competition among analysts. The analysts' rationale for resisting widespread coordination is that they consider themselves subject matter experts.

Beyond the thicket of coordination and collaboration, the analysis process becomes tough to execute when the office finds that several consumers demand attention all at once. When this occurs, the office's cradle-to-grave, face-to-face, and surge-flexible process becomes overwhelmed. One subject acknowledged that the tension between higher and lower echelon consumers and the tension between two or more concurrent contingencies gave them the most concern. Consumers typically ask the office's leaders to intervene when they believe the office is not meeting their requirements. As a result, the analyst can expect to have to shift priorities and perform many tasks under a great deal of stress.

Collaboration and Competition

Collaboration. If analysts choose not to collaborate with other Community experts, then the SIO may force them to do so during the coordination and review process. Managers want analysts to verify the validity of all of their information in a manner similar to the way that they feel compelled to check and verify human-resource information. They also need to confirm source reliability, be able to articulate the method they used to derive the information, and to confirm the information's contextual accuracy.

Competition. Collaboration among intelligence analysts is always a problem because analysts, like many school children, tend to be competitive with each other. The acknowledged lack of coordination within DIA is not a new or exceptional phenomenon. New analysts may not know who to talk to on a particular subject or where to go to get useful information. A more senior mentor or manager can usually provide the analysts with that kind of information, but the exchange of information between analysts doesn't normally happen in the unsupervised work environment. Analysts are very competitive within the office and especially with other agencies in the IC. There is a strong desire to publish first, a tendency that inhibits full disclosure to competing analysts. Other intelligence agencies usually have more resources than DIA and can report an item more quickly than DIA. From another perspective, one subject reflected on how analysis was done at the CIA many years ago. He said CIA analysts would initiate collaboration when necessary and had occasional meetings to share information. They had mixed luck with people external to their organization. Academics sometimes refused to talk to them. One time an ambassador was reluctant to talk with them. Overall, he concludes that there was very little collaboration "back then." He provided two examples:

First, all cross-office work was called "collaboration-by-staple." One person would write the first half of the paper and the other person from a different office wrote the second half. A person from a neutral third office would edit the entire paper. Then they would staple it together and send it out. A more truly collaborative work environment would have made it easier for the analysts to bounce ideas off of each other and test their assumptions. Back then, everything was much more competitive even than today.

Second, message traffic came into the office mainly in paper format, rather than the electronic format of today. One clever analyst would come into the office each day much earlier than anyone else. He would review the message traffic, take the good papers, and then produce analysis on interesting topics that he would present later in the morning to his office leaders. Others in the office would be left to report on the remaining message traffic that was less interesting. In this subject's view, the office leaders unfortunately let this go on without intervention.

Summary

Good analysts are "focused freethinkers." Nevertheless, "out-of-the-box"-type thinking needs to be tempered by using an informal, disciplined thought process and collaborating with other analysts The scientific method is a streamlined process that ensures the analyst doesn't wander too far. Use of information is problem-dependent. There is, however, a general consensus among our subjects that analysts should use everything they can get their hands on. Analysts also need to assess the reliability of their sources and at the same time, protect the identity of sensitive sources. Collaboration tends to vary by organization and by issue. Collaboration tends to be better between analysts within DIA than between analysts from different parent organizations such as between CIA and DIA. There tends to be a competitive nature among analysts to be the first to publish their product.

MISSION ACCOMPLISHMENT

The mission accomplishment category examines the analyst's definition of success, and proceeds to secure an estimate of the percentage of time analysts believe they are successful.

Definition of Success

All of our subjects agreed that success is a difficult concept to define. Our subjects did, however, agree that it might be possible. First, success is positive feedback from consumers. If they do not provide explicit positive feedback, then the analysis shop can look for indirect indicators. For example, if the consumers keep coming back for more analysis, then analysts consider their products successful. Another informal way of measuring success was to count complaints.

Second, an intelligence analysis success occurs when a unit that is known to depend on DIA products completes its military operation successfully. If, however, there is loss of life during a mission, then the analysts are greatly disturbed. Their product may have in some way contributed to the lack of success for the military operation.

Third, success is obtaining an expanding budget and a growing workforce. These developments indicate that the topic focus is perceived as interesting by agency leadership. One subject labeled this type of success as "bureaucratic success."

Fourth, success to some analysts means that evidence indicates that they are able to look at things in the open sources and link them in ways others could not envision. The analyst would observe a situation, notice a trend, and take a position on a tough issue. The following descriptions are examples of good analysis written during the 1980s:

- The analyst's bosses didn't want a paper on the future of Lebanon written because it was a tough issue. When the analyst completed the paper, the director of the agency wanted to see it. The bosses fought among themselves to see who would take it to him. After reading it, the director wanted 20 copies to give to the Secretary of State.

- An analyst identified a high level of tension among the cultural groups living in Yugoslavia. The analyst reasoned that strong suppression was holding these cultures in check. When Tito dies, the analyst warned, "Look Out!" This example indicates that estimative studies should not be dismissed out of hand.[16]

- An analyst identified problems in African cities because of a certain mix of people living there. The paper predicted that similar problems would happen in suburbs as the suburbs began to get the same mix of people. As it turned out, the analyst was correct.

Fifth, a representative from one office defined success as a function of terrorist attacks. If no terrorist attacks happened, then they would consider themselves successful. However, terrorist attacks could potentially happen anytime, and if one happens, then the shop would consider itself unsuccessful.

Sixth, analysts in general put out a lot of paper and products in support of military "force protection," and to support the senior intelligence officers (J-2s) of the JCS and of the Unified Commands. DIA analysts consider themselves successful if their consumers change their behavior by doing things differently as a result of information provided.

Percent Successful

Study subjects clearly struggled to answer the question of how often they are successful. One subject said he had no answer: "Sometimes you will never know whether or not you were successful." He could confirm in any given case that no negative response had come from stakeholders, yet he could not be sure that the consumers considered their products successful. One subject said success for his office was at 90 percent. However, he could not elaborate.

---

[16] Perhaps the clearest exposition of how estimative intelligence can be accomplished in a way to discourage the work's being easily dismissed is provided by Isaac Ben-Israel in "Philosophy and Methodology of Intelligence: The Logic of Estimate Process," *Intelligence and National Security* 4, no. 4 (October 1989): 660-718.

One subject said that by his personal definition, all analyses were successful. His criterion for success was to go beyond the status quo, to clearly articulate views to real consumers, and to establish a feedback loop on utility of products. He admitted there was no readily accepted measure and no guidance concerning success. One way for an analyst to be successful was to get his work published. At least that would get his boss off his back for a certain amount of time! Still another subject said all products were in some sense successful. To be successful, he continued, it is important for someone to look at the products. One possible way to measure success is to count the number of electronic hits on a particular document on a database. If consumers are asking questions, then analysts can feel they are being helpful. An informal summary metric, then, is the measure of information flow out of the office.

Summary

Intelligence analysis supports DoD organizations and warfighter operations. Mission success is positive feedback from consumers or a successful completion of military operations. Bureaucratic success, on the other hand, results in more money to spend and more analysts to do the job. Analysts consider themselves successful if their consumers changed their behavior based on the information they provided to them. For example, successful analysts warn unit commanders of a possible terrorist attack and as a result of their work, the commander takes the appropriate steps to improve unit force protection.

STRATEGIES FOR SUCCESSFUL INTELLIGENCE ANALYSIS

"What is good intelligence analysis?"

Good or useful intelligence analysis may be best defined by its opposite. Bad intelligence does not specify what the threat is or how it will manifest itself. For example, the analyst may conclude there will be a 50 percent chance of a chemical weapons attack against the U.S. in the next 10 years. That conclusion is not meaningful or helpful to planners and users of intelligence.[17] In another example, the analyst may conclude that all ports are dangerous to U.S. ships. This analysis is impractical because ships have to use ports occasionally.

In positive terms, good intelligence analysis enlightens commanders or consumers. It doesn't necessarily have formal probabilities. Instead it communicates to the commander some level of likelihood. For example, if the commander implements plan X, then a terrorist group in this location is likely to react in the following manner. This information is

---

[17] Richards Heuer, 155, reproduces a table illustrating the different numerical probabilities that intelligence analysts and consumers associate with common word descriptions of probability. The message is that neither form of presentation expresses probability in a reliable fashion. The table appeared originally in Sherman Kent, "Words of Estimated Probability," in Donald P. Steury, ed., *Sherman Kent and the Board of National Estimates: Collected Essays* (CIA: Center for the Study of Intelligence, 1994), 133-137.

valuable to the commander because it gives him or her the opportunity to change plans based on the analysis. It enlightens the commander of the current situation. Good intelligence analysis takes a position on an issue. Some current intelligence products fail to say anything of substance because they use normative words such as "would," "could," "should," "will likely," "might, "may," and "can be." These products have limited value to the consumer. A remaining question is "How can intelligence products be made more useful?"

Good analysts use quantitative data when appropriate. Over time there has been a rise in the use of statistics in intelligence products. One subject observed that many years ago analysts rarely used statistics in their analysis. Then, some analysts used statistics, but they didn't write about it in their papers. He recognized statements made in the paper that would require use of a certain structured technique. He would call the author(s) to inquire about the technique. Usually, he was right. The author(s) had used the technique. After a while, some authors put the data in the appendix of their paper so others might replicate their work. Then, analysts began to put their statistical analysis in the text portion of their papers. These products became more like academic research papers than they had been in the past. Analysts tend to respond favorably to any form of rigor in intelligence products.

Richard K. Betts says intelligence failures are most often caused by decisionmakers who consume the products of intelligence service. The use of intelligence depends less on the bureaucracy than on intellect. Therefore, one can only get modest improvement by altering the analytic system.[18] Jay T. Young, on the other hand, sees barriers to more effective analysis that could be corrected by managerial, personnel, and training reform. He believes that an overhaul of the U.S. intelligence community's analysis effort can improve its effectiveness while reducing its overall size and cost.[19]

In government work, the applied nature of intelligence production would seem to offer the opportunity to develop and apply consistent measures of productivity and quality, just because the products are indeed used by specific consumers. If this is true, then there is room to bring "operations research" into play as well as the Baldrige criteria, to encourage the development and collection of carefully codified, surrogate measures of productivity and quality. Successful use of these tools does not remove from the manager the task of decisionmaking but rather it requires of him or her rather different kinds of decisions. In other words, using operations research tools provides managers with extra insight into their particular subject and hence leads them into much more difficult but fruitful areas. Consultants with scholarly backgrounds could come into the intelligence analysis work environment and make vast improvement to the intelligence analysis capability using such tools to assist them, in the author's opinion.

------

[18] Richard K. Betts, "Analysis, War, and Decision: Why Intelligence Failures are Inevitable," *World Politics* 31, no. 1 (October 1978): 61-89

[19] Jay T. Young, "US Intelligence Assessment in a Changing World: The Need for Reform," *Intelligence and National Security* 8, no. 2 (April 1993): 125-1390

QUESTIONS FOR FUTURE RESEARCH

Our subjects offered the following questions for future study:

1. Does DIA prepare analysts for their work by acquainting them with the use of analytic tools? Does DIA provide adequate analysis training?

2. What are the implications of the substantial difference between the ideal way for doing analysis and the way DIA analysts actually do it? For example, data are often contradictory and vague. They do not point in any particular direction. Yet the analyst knows he must draw conclusions at the end of the study. Can anyone conclude anything from such data?

3. If you could have any tool (real or imaginary) to help do your analysis better, what would that tool be? For example, some people like having fancy graphics in their papers or as part of their analysis.

4. What attitudes characterize DIA analysts? Do DIA analysts have a tendency to be more receptive to collaboration, or more competitive than government analysts in other agencies?

NOT AN END, BUT A BEGINNING

This report does not represent the end of the intelligence analysis benchmarking study; rather it creates a platform for a wide range of beginnings. The approaches identified in this report will come to life by being shared, debated, and implemented in the context of Department of Defense and Intelligence Community realities. Then, where appropriate, they may be used and expanded upon. Intelligence analysts throughout the intelligence community can establish their own analysis networks and working groups to share their own best practices and lessons learned with each other.

	Benchmarking Offices				
	1	2	3	4	5
1. Does your office leadership support analysis process?	Y/N	Y	Y	Y	Y/N
Usually leader assigns tasks		Y	Y		
Usually analysts perform self-generated tasks	Y		Y		Y
Analysts usually respond to crises			Y	Y	
Little or no interaction during analysis process	Y	Y			Y
Some interaction if asked			Y	Y	
Tend to put products on electronic media	Y	Y			
Tend to put products in many different forms			Y	Y	Y
Formal feedback and coordination process at end	Y	Y	Y		Y
Informal feedback prior to finished product				Y	Y
2. Does your office have a written strategic plan?	N	N	N	N	N
Able to meet future capability challenges	N	Y	Y	Y/N	Y
Able to meet future issues challenges	N	Y	Y	Y/N	Y
Recorded lessons learned	N	N	Y/N	Y/N	N

	Benchmarking Offices				
	1	2	3	4	5
Use academic or professional sources	Y	Y	Y	Y	Y
3. Do your consumers support the analysis process?	Y/N	Y	Y	Y	Y
Requirements through COLISEUM & phone calls	Y	Y	Y	Y	Y
Little or no interaction during the analysis process	Y		Y		Y
Some informal interaction if appropriate		Y		Y	
Electronic publications and/or hard copies	Y	Y		Y	Y
Use multiple methods to market products			Y		
Little or no formal feedback	Y	Y	Y/N	Y/N	Y/N
4. Do you measure your analysis performance?	N	N	N	N	N
Lack of negative feedback from consumers			Y	Y	
Consumers find product useful			Y	Y	
Analysts show improvement over time		Y			
Don't track forecast accuracy					Y
Use or plan to use standard metrics	N	N	N	N	N
5. Do you have the right people and resources?	Y/N	Y	Y	Y	Y
Need to think across interdisciplinary boundaries	Y				
Need balance between computer skills & being SME		Y			Y
Need diverse mix of experiences			Y		Y
Need military operations experiences				Y	
Want analysts to develop and use toolbox	Y	Y	Y	Y	Y
6. Do you have a formal process for doing analysis?	N	N	N	N	N
Does informal process inhibit good analysis?	Y	Y/N	N	Y/N	
Use all information you can get		Y			
Use creativity to make-up for resource shortages	Y				
Use open-source data more	Y	Y	Y		
Information use is problem dependent			Y	Y	
Assess reliability of sources					Y
Do your analysts collaborate with other analysts?	N	Y/N	Y/N	Y	Y/N
7. Does your office make a positive contribution?	Y	Y	Y	Y	Y
Use consumer feedback		Y		Y	Y
Contribute to mission accomplishment		Y		Y	
Expand budget and grow workforce	Y				
Consumer changes behavior based on analysis			Y		
Successful most of time	Y	Y	Y	Y	

Responses to Interview Questions, by Office.

The purpose of the matrix is to summarize what was learned during the interviews. The author constructed the matrix after the interviews took place. All of the responses in a single column are directly related back to a specific interviewee. If the respondent referenced a specific item in his response and indicated yes or no to that item, then that response is recorded on the line related to that item in the matrix. If the box is blank, then the respondent did not refer to that item in his response. In other words, the author is uncertain what the respondent would say concerning the item in the matrix. The interviewer asked each subject the first question in the series of items directly. As a result, each box for the first question in the series of items is complete. No item in the matrix has a completely blank line because someone had to refer to the item in his response in order to get the item listed in the matrix. The matrix provides a frequency count of items mentioned in response to the topic being discussed.

BIBLIOGRAPHY

Allison, Graham. *Essence of Decision: Explaining the Cuban Missile Crisis*, Little Brown, 1971.

Ben-Israel, Isaac. "Philosophy and Methodology of Intelligence: The Logic of Estimate Process." *Intelligence and National Security* 4, no. 4 (October 1989): 660-718.

Betts, Richard. "Analysis, War and Decision: Why Intelligence Failures Are Inevitable." *World Politics* 31, no. 1 (October 1978): 61-89.

Brei, William S. *Getting Intelligence Right: The Power of Logical Procedure*. Occasional Paper Number Two. Washington, DC: JMIC, January 1996.

Clark, Robert M., *Intelligence Analysis: Estimation and Prediction*. Baltimore: MD: American Literary Press, 1996.

Folker, Robert D., Jr. *Intelligence Analysis in Theater Joint Intelligence Centers: An Experiment in Applying Structured Methods*. Occasional Paper Number Seven. Washington, DC: JMIC, January 2000.

Heuer, Richards J., Jr. *Psychology of Intelligence Analysis*. Washington, DC: Center for the Study of Intelligence, 1999.

Hogarth, Robin. *Judgement and Choice*, John Wiley, 1987.

Jervis, Robert. *Perception and Misperception in International Politics*. Princeton, NJ: Princeton University Press, 1977.

Jones, Morgan. *The Thinker's Toolkit: 14 Powerful Techniques for Problem Solving*. New York: Random House, Inc., 1995.

Kam, Ephraim. *Surprise Attack*. Cambridge, MA: Harvard University Press, 1988.

Krizan, Lisa. *Intelligence Essentials for Everyone*. Occasional Paper Number Six. Washington, DC: JMIC, June 1999.

Kuhn, Thomas. *The Structure of Scientific Revolutions*. Chicago, IL: University of Chicago Press, 1970.

May, Ernest. *"Lessons" of the Past: The Use and Misuse of History in American Foreign Policy*. New York: Oxford University Press, 1973.

Merom, Gil. "The 1962 Cuban Intelligence Estimate: A Methodical Perspective," *Intelligence and National Security* 14, no. 3 (Autumn 1999): 48-80.

Platt, John R. "Strong Inference," *Science* 146, no. 3642 (16 October 1964): 347-353.

Russo, J. Edward, and Paul J. H. Shoemaker. *Decision Traps: Ten Barriers to Brilliant Decision-Making and How to Overcome Them*. New York: Simon and Schuster, 1989.

Young, Jay T. "US Intelligence Assessment in a Changing World: The Need for Reform," *Intelligence and National Security* 8, no. 2 (April 1993): 125-139.

ABOUT THE AUTHORS

David T. Moore is a senior technical leader at the National Security Agency. During 18 years of Intelligence Community service he has completed a variety of assignments in the Washington, DC area and overseas. These assignments enabled Mr. Moore to earn credentials in technical communications analysis, intelligence analysis, and intelligence research. He has created and taught intelligence analysis courses for NSA's National Cryptological School as well as for other government agencies. His most recent assignment was in the Art and Science of Analysis organization where his work focused on improving methodologies for intelligence analysis. He holds a B.A. in sociology/anthropology from Washington and Lee University and an M.S. in Strategic Intelligence from the Joint Military Intelligence College.

Lisa Krizan is a senior technical leader at the National Security Agency. A self-described "intelligence brat," she was introduced to the field by her father, Col. Allen J. Montecino, Jr., USAF, retired. Through diverse experience in intelligence support and production assignments, Ms. Krizan has earned credentials in technical communications analysis, intelligence research, and foreign language analysis, and has created and taught intelligence analysis courses for the National Cryptologic School. She received a B.S. degree in Business and Management from the University of Maryland and an M.S. in Strategic Intelligence from the Joint Military Intelligence College. Her master's thesis, "Benchmarking the Intelligence Process for the Private Sector" was the result of combining her studies in best business practices with her Intelligence Community work. Ms. Krizan is also the author of *Intelligence Essentials for Everyone*, published in June 1999 by the JMIC as Occasional Paper Number Six.

Mr. Moore and Ms. Krizan's current work on core competencies arose from their continuing advocacy for best practices in intelligence analysis, as members of the Art and Science of Analysis organization.

CORE COMPETENCIES FOR INTELLIGENCE ANALYSIS AT THE NATIONAL SECURITY AGENCY

David T. Moore and Lisa Krizan

Seekers of Wisdom first need sound intelligence.

— *Heraclitus[1]*

What makes an intelligence analyst successful in the profession? This question strikes at the heart of the National Foreign Intelligence Community's mission to provide actionable information to national leaders and decisionmakers. The imperative to answer this question stems from two types of pressures, external and internal. Externally, the component agencies face a world that demands responsiveness, agility, and flexibility.[2] Internally, they are charged with transforming outdated Cold War organizational structure, mentality, and methods.[3] This paper argues that, at least at the National Security Agency, identifying core analytic competencies that can be translated into managerial strategies is the surest way to ensure that intelligence analysts are successful.

As a member of the Intelligence Community (IC), the National Security Agency (NSA) is now pursuing an ambitious campaign to modernize its intelligence production mission and to mold its workforce accordingly.[4] Part of the modernization campaign is a new organizational model that places all intelligence analysts under the purview of an analytic deployment service. In this paradigm, individual analysts are assigned to specific production lines based on the capabilities of the former and the needs of the latter. However, for this model to work, staffers need to know what assets the analysts in the work force possess. Similarly, when intelligence agencies use precious few hiring allocations to bring in new intelligence analysts, they must maximize those opportunities, and only hire qualified personnel. But what is a qualified intelligence analyst?

---

[1] From Brooks Haxton, translator, *Fragments, the Collected Wisdom of Heraclitus* (New York: Penguin, 2001), 33.

[2] John Gannon and others, National Intelligence Council, *Global Trends 2015: A Dialogue About the Future with Nongovernment Experts* (Washington DC: National Foreign Intelligence Board, 2000), 41, URL: *http://www.cia.gov/cia/publications/globaltrends2015/;* hereafter cited as National Intelligence Council. For other views of security threats to America see also Loch Johnson, *Bombs, Bugs, Drugs, and Thugs: Intelligence and America's Quest for Security* (New York: New York University Press, 2000); and Robert D. Kaplan, *The Coming Anarchy: Shattering the Dreams of the Post-Cold War* (New York: Random House, 2000).

[3] George W. Bush, "National Security Presidential Directive 5," 9 May 2001. This directive instructs the Director of Central Intelligence to conduct a comprehensive review of U.S. intelligence. The order gives the DCI a broad mandate to "challenge the status quo."

[4] See URL: *http://www.nsa.gov/releases/nsa_new_enterprise_team_recommendations.pdf,* 1 October 1999, 16, accessed 3 November 2001. In this document, it is implicit that the Director, NSA recognizes that the agency's responsibility for the "production of signals intelligence" extends beyond "technical analysis of data" to "all-source" analysis of the context and implications of those data, especially but not exclusively for use within the agency itself.

In this paper the authors propose a set of functional core competencies for intelligence analysis, shown in the figure below, which provides a starting point for answering fundamental questions about the nature of ideal intelligence professionals, and how analysts who share these ideals can go about doing their work. Keeping in mind the complex nature of the threats to U.S. national security, we argue that the strategy for deploying intelligence analysts and for carrying out intelligence production must become more rigorous to keep pace with 21st Century foes, and to defeat them.

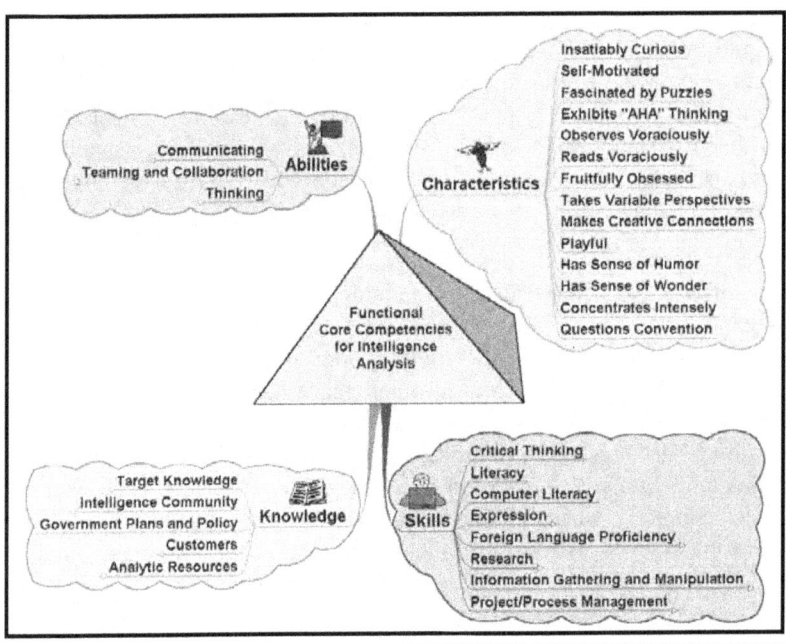

Functional core competencies for intelligence analysis..

The authors began exploring the art and science of intelligence analysis at their agency as part of a corporate initiative to add rigor to its analytic practice. Comments presented here on analytic thinking, its associated culture and processes, and its related technologies reflect conversations with intelligence experts both within and outside of government, and observation of analysts considered by their peers to be successful. We realized that definitions and descriptions of common characteristics, skills, knowledge, and abilities required for successful intelligence analysis were lacking, not only within our own agency but across the field of intelligence. We developed a set of functional core competencies for intelligence analysis that seem to apply across the intelligence profession in the government setting, not just for the types of analysis done at NSA. Our work has been reviewed by personnel in our agency as well as by individuals outside government, including academic experts on intelligence and intelligence analysis.[5] They have made helpful suggestions for our model of functional core competencies.

Sherman Kent, who helped shape the national peacetime intelligence community, argues that intelligence requires its own literature. According to Kent, a key purpose of this literature is to advance the discipline of intelligence. Kent believed "[as] long as this discipline lacks a literature, its method, its vocabulary, its body of doctrine, and even its fundamental theory run the risk of never reaching full maturity."[6] Through the publication of articles on analysis and subsequent discussion, "original synthesis of all that has gone before" occurs.[7] In keeping with Kent's mandate to develop an intelligence literature that provokes discussion and further methodological development, we seek comment and further discussion among scholars of intelligence studies.

DEFINITIONS AND CONTEXT

Intelligence refers to information that meets the stated or understood needs of policymakers.... All intelligence is information; not all information is intelligence.

— *Mark Lowenthal*[8]

Intelligence is timely, actionable information that helps policymakers, decisionmakers, and military leaders perform their national security functions. The intelligence business itself depends on professional competencies, what John Gannon, former Chairman of the National Intelligence Council, refers to as "skills and expertise." He notes that "this means people—people in whom we will need to invest more to deal with the array of complex challenges we face over the next generation."[9] Analysis is the process by which

---

[5] The authors wish to acknowledge individuals within the Department of Defense who challenged our ideas and critiqued our work. Thanks also are due to James Holden-Rhodes, University of New Mexico; Robert Heibel, Mercyhurst College; Hugo Keesing, Joint Military Intelligence Training Center; Marilyn Peterson, Financial Analysis Coordinator, New Jersey Division of Criminal Justice; Adam Pode, formerly of Mercyhurst College; Robert David Steele, CEO, Open Source Solutions; and Russell Swenson, Joint Military Intelligence College. Colleagues in the international Generic Intelligence Training Initiative, sponsored by the U.S. Drug Enforcement Administration, also provided valuable comments.

[6] *Sherman Kent and the Board of National Estimates: Collected Essays,* Donald P. Steury, ed., (Washington DC: Center for the Study of Intelligence, Central Intelligence Agency, 1994), 14.

[7] See Sherman Kent, "The Need for an Intelligence Literature," *Studies in Intelligence*, Spring, 1955 (reprinted in Studies in Intelligence, 45th Anniversary Special Edition, Washington DC: Government Printing Office, 2001), 1-11.

[8] Mark M. Lowenthal, *Intelligence: From Secrets to Policy* (Washington, DC: CQ Press, 2000), 1-2.

people transform information into intelligence. Ultimately, analysis leads to synthesis and effective persuasion, or, less pointedly, estimation.[10] It does so by breaking down large problems into a number of smaller ones, involving "close examination of related items of information to determine the extent to which they confirm, supplement, or contradict each other and thus to establish probabilities and relationships."[11]

Since the advent of the Information Age, "[collecting] information is less of a problem and verifying is more of one."[12] Thus the role of analysis becomes more vital as the supply of information available to consumers from every type of source, proven and unproven, multiplies exponentially. Intelligence analysts are more than merely another information source, more than collectors and couriers of information to consumers. Further,

> [the] images that are sometimes evoked of policymakers surfing the Net themselves, in direct touch with their own information sources, are very misleading. Most of the time, as [policymakers'] access to information multiplies, their need for processing, if not analysis, will go up. If collection is easier, selection will be harder.[13]

At its best, the results of intelligence analysis provide just the right information permitting national leaders "to make wise decisions—all presented with accuracy, timeliness, and clarity."[14] The intelligence provided must "contain hard-hitting, focused analysis relevant to current policy issues....Therefore, analysis of raw information has the most impact on the decisionmaker and [therefore] producing high-quality analytical product should be the highest priority for intelligence agencies."[15]

Intelligence is judged, then, on its usefulness. But what criteria define "useful?" Amos Kovacs asserts that useful intelligence makes a "difference" to policymakers.[16] There is also an expectation that intelligence should be unbiased, although analysts with concerns

---

[9] Director of Central Intelligence National Security Advisory Panel, *Strategic Investment Plan for Intelligence Community Analysis* (Washington DC: Central Intelligence Agency, 2000), URL: *http://www.cia.gov/cia/publications/unclass_sip/index.html*, 11, accessed 29 September 2001.

[10] Lisa Krizan, *Intelligence Essentials for Everyone*, Joint Military College Occasional Paper Number Six (Washington DC: Joint Military Intelligence College, 1999), 29.

[11] R. H. Mathams, "The Intelligence Analyst's Notebook," in *Strategic Intelligence: Theory and Application*, 2d. ed. Douglas H. Dearth and R. Thomas Goodden, eds. (Washington, DC: Joint Military Intelligence Training Center, 1995), 88.

[12] R. H. Mathams, 88.

[13] R. H. Mathams, 88; Gregory F. Treverton, *Reshaping National Intelligence For an Age of Information* (Cambridge, UK; Cambridge University Press, 2001), 10.

[14] Loch K. Johnson, "Analysis for a New Age," *Intelligence and National Security* 11, no. 4 (October 1996): 658.

[15] Kevin P. Stack, "Competitive Intelligence," *Intelligence and National Security* 13, no. 4 (Winter 1998): 194.

about outcomes do influence the product by selecting which inputs to analyze.[17] Finally, as Michael Turner points out, analysts "from below" now join senior government officials in "setting the analytical agenda."[18] All policymakers and their subordinates are free to reject intelligence findings, no matter how persuasively argued they may be.

To say that policymakers may dismiss intelligence that doesn't support their presuppositions and policy objectives is to tell only half the story. There may be numerous reasons why policymakers do not accept intelligence. Gregory Treverton, former Vice-Chair of the National Intelligence Council, indicates that intelligence is ignored both when it brings inconvenient news and when it offers nothing new. In writing about the U.S. policy failures of the first Bush administration during the Balkan crisis, Treverton wonders, "If, in retrospect, the intelligence seems on the mark, did the policy failure derive from intelligence unheeded, or was the intelligence heeded but either not new or not really actionable?"[19]

Treverton adds that intelligence must anticipate the needs of policy. "By the time policy knows what it needs to know, it is usually too late for intelligence to respond by developing new sources or cranking up its analytic capacity."[20] A former policymaker himself, he asserts that intelligence is useful to policy at three stages during the life of an issue:

- If the policymakers are prescient, when the issue is just beginning; however there is likely to be little intelligence on the issue at that point.
- When the issue is "ripe for decision." Here policymakers want intelligence that permits alternatives to be considered; however, intelligence often is only able to provide background information necessary for understanding the issue.
- When the policymakers have made up their minds on the issue, but only if intelligence supports their view. They will be uninterested or even hostile when it does not support their view.[21]

These limitations notwithstanding, Treverton suggests that policymakers can and should establish a symbiotic relationship with the intelligence analysts who advise them:

> [If] you call them in, face to face, they will understand how much you know, and you'll have a chance to calibrate them. You'll learn more in fifteen minutes than you'd have imagined. And you'll also begin to target those analysts to your concerns and your sense of the issue.[22]

---

[16]Amos Kovacs, "Using Intelligence," *Intelligence and National Security* 12, no. 4 (October 1997): 148.

[17]Lowenthal, 4.

[18]Michael A. Turner, "Setting Analytical Priorities in U.S. Intelligence," *International Journal of Intelligence and Counterintelligence* 9, no. 3 (Fall 1996): 314.

[19]Treverton, 178.

[20]Treverton, 179.

[21]Treverton, 183-185.

Similarly, the analyst has responsibilities to the policymaker. In commenting on this relationship, Sherman Kent asserts

> [intelligence] performs a service function. Its job is to see that the doers are generally well informed; its job is to stand behind them with a book opened at the right page to call their attention to the stubborn fact they may be neglecting, and—at their request—to analyze alternative courses without indicating choice.[23]

In Kent's view, the intelligence analyst is required to ensure, tenaciously, that policymakers view those "right" pages, even when they may not wish to do so.

MEASURING SUCCESS IN INTELLIGENCE ANALYSIS

Intelligence must be measured to be valued, so let us take the initiative and ask our management, [and] the users, to evaluate us and our products.

— Jan P. Herring[24]

Any observer can expect that a successful intelligence analyst will have certain personal characteristics that tend to foster dedication to the work and quality of results. Such an analyst will also have specific abilities, skills, and knowledge to perform intelligence work. Finally such an analyst will have productive relationships with consumers. But how can success in intelligence analysis be measured?

Measures of success have been based on job performance, including numbers of reports issued; volumes of raw data processed; or degree of consumer reliance on, or satisfaction with, products or services. However, these are measurements of outcome, only one facet of success. When analysis follows a rigorous process that allows an analyst to "add value" to information, and that results in timely, actionable intelligence used by consumers, then it may be judged successful. Thus, an assessment of success may be made by balancing measures of two basic criteria: intelligence process (processing and adding value to information) and intelligence product (meeting consumer needs). As depicted in the figure below, each can keep the other in balance, curbing any tendency toward "analysis paralysis"[25] on one side, and countering an assembly-line mindset on the other.

---

[22] Treverton, 191.

[23] Sherman Kent, *Strategic Intelligence for American World Policy* (Princeton: Princeton University Press, 1949), 182.

[24] Jan P. Herring, *Measuring the Effectiveness of Competitive Intelligence: Assessing and Communicating CI's Value to Your Organization* (Alexandria, VA: Society of Competitive Intelligence Professionals, 1996), 63.

Rigorous Analysis

- Holistic
- Competitive
- Adds Value
- Highest Cognitive Level
- Collaborative

Sound Management

- Customer Relations
- Community Relations
- Resource Allocation
- Organization of Work
- Empowering Analysts
- Valuing Analysts

Convey Intelligence

- Analytic Conclusions
- Decision Points
- Implications of Choices

Meet/Anticipate Customer Needs

- Readiness
- Timeliness
- Objectivity
- Usability
- Relevance

An intelligence evaluation scheme.

Intelligence Process

Successful intelligence analysis is a holistic process involving both "art" and "science." Intuitive abilities, inherent aptitudes, rigorously applied skills, and acquired knowledge together enable analysts to work problems in a multidimensional manner, thereby avoiding the pitfalls of both scientism and adventurism. The former occurs when scientific methodology is excessively relied upon to reveal the "truth"; the latter occurs when "inspiration [is] unsupported by rigorous analysis."[26]

---

[25] One potential pitfall of the analytic profession is the tendency to pursue analysis for its own sake, continually seeking more information, becoming locked into analysis and failing to reach conclusions. Rigorous methodology that emphasizes adding value to information and making it actionable for a specific consumer can break the cycle of such paralysis.

[26] Steven R. Mann, "Chaos Theory and Strategic Thought," *Parameters* 22, no. 3 (Autumn 1992): 67. Quoted in MSgt Robert D. Folker, Jr., *Intelligence Analysis in Theater Joint Intelligence Centers: An Experiment in Applying Structured Methods*, Occasional Paper Number Seven (Washington DC: Joint Military Intelligence College, 2000), 13.

A vital contributor to the analytic process is a spirit of competition, both within an intelligence-producing agency and especially between intelligence agencies. There is a tendency for analysts working together to develop a common mindset. This trap occurs typically when analysts fail to question their assumptions about their role in the intelligence process and about the target. The Council on Foreign Relations' independent task force on the future of U.S. intelligence recommends that "competitive or redundant analysis be encouraged" precisely for these reasons.[27]

Successful analysis adds value—to the information itself, to institutional knowledge, to fellow intelligence professionals, to the process, and to the institution or unit itself—in terms of reputation and the degree to which good analytic practices endure despite changes in target, consumer, and personnel. Successful analysts are those whose work, whenever possible goes to the level of making judgments or estimating. The analysts' risks in doing so are carefully calculated, for successful analysts rely on critical thinking. Nor do successful analysts settle for the first answer their analysis reveals. Rather they employ rigorous methods to push beyond the obvious conclusions. However, tendencies toward arrogance in trend-spotting analysis are tempered by self-awareness of biases and assumptions, strengths and weaknesses. And most importantly, successful analysts collaborate at every opportunity. Such measures ensure that analytic results, even if controversial, remain grounded in reality.

What role does management play in ensuring analytic success? First and foremost, management effectively uses financial and political capital to ensure that analysts have access to consumers, and to the resources they require to answer those consumers' intelligence needs. This includes the organization of the work itself, allocation of materiel and personnel, and coordination with consumers and other producers. When management is successful, the analyst has the necessary tools and the correct information for successful intelligence analysis. Good morale among analytic personnel becomes an indicator of effective management. A good understanding of the unit's mission and the analysts' own satisfaction with his or her performance naturally produces a feeling of empowerment and a belief that the organization places great value on analytic talent.

Intelligence Product

The products of successful analysis convey intelligence that meets or anticipates the consumer's needs; these products reveal analytic conclusions, not the methods used to derive them. Intelligence products are successful if they arm the decisionmaker, policymaker or military leader with the information and context—the answers—needed to win on his or her playing field. Such intelligence enables consumers to be more effective by making them smarter than they were before, smarter than the people they play with, and smarter than those they play against. Successful intelligence enables consumers to outwit

---

[27] Council on Foreign Relations, *Making Intelligence Smarter: The Future of U.S. Intelligence: A Report of an Independent Task Force*, 11, URL: *http://www.fas.org/irp/efr.html*, accessed 4 June 2001.

opponents, protect U.S. persons, bring aid to the nation's allies, or to judge levels of trust. It does so by revealing decision points, actions or choices available to a consumer, and the implications of choosing one over another.

Yet, consumers rarely acknowledge explicitly the role that good intelligence plays in their own success. While they may be quick to bring intelligence failures to the attention of the producing organization, consumers do not always give feedback on successful outcomes enabled by intelligence. Thus intelligence analysts and their management historically have looked within the production organization for ways to measure success, falling into the trap of "bean-counting." But there is a better way.

> **Readiness:** Intelligence systems must be responsive to existing and contingent intelligence requirements of consumers at all levels.
>
> **Timeliness:** Intelligence must be delivered while the content is still actionable under the consumer's circumstances.
>
> **Accuracy:** All sources and data must be evaluated for the possibility of technical error, misperception, and hostile efforts to mislead.
>
> **Objectivity:** All judgments must be evaluated for the possibility of deliberate distortions and manipulations due to self-interest.
>
> **Usability:** All intelligence output must be in a form that facilitates ready comprehension and immediate application. Intelligence products must be compatible with the consumer's capabilities for receiving, manipulating, protecting, and storing the product.
>
> **Relevance:** Information must be selected and organized for its applicability to a consumer's requirements, with potential consequences and significance of the information made explicit to the consumer's circumstances.

Measures of success for intelligence products[28]

Six "underlying ideas or core values" for intelligence analysis, identified by William Brei for operational-level intelligence, and shown in the figure above, establish the analyst's "essential work processes."[29] Since they are defined in terms of the consumer, they also can be used as a checklist to rate the quality of products provided to the consumer. Brei asserts that they "provide specific qualitative objectives for managers and leaders, and a framework for standards against which intelligence services should be judged."[30] While qualitative feedback from consumers aids evaluation of some of these objectives, the absence of consumer input does not prevent their being used in self-evaluation.

---

[28] William S. Brei, Captain, USAF, *Getting Intelligence Right: The Power of Logical Procedure*, Occasional Paper Number Two (Washington DC: Joint Military Intelligence College, 1996), 6.

[29] Brei, 6.

[30] Brei, 5.

The principles of Readiness and Timeliness evaluate the intelligence service's basic ability to perform intelligence production. These two principles are limiting factors affecting what the producer can do to "achieve accurate data, objective judgments, usable formats, and relevant products."[31] Once production Readiness and Timeliness are evaluated, the other four of Brei's fundamental principles then can be arranged in a checklist or a series of questions about intelligence products. Typical questions might include:

- Was the reported intelligence accurate? (*Accuracy*)
- Are there any distortions in the reported judgments? (*Objectivity*)
- Is the reported intelligence actionable? Does it facilitate ready comprehension? (*Usability*)
- Does it support the consumer's mission? Is it applicable to the consumer's requirements? Has its significance been made explicit? (*Relevance*)

These four principles also overlap, and poor quality in one can affect the quality of another. Brei asserts that accurate data provide the foundation for subsequent objective judgments, and the expression of objective judgments in a usable form provides much of the basis of a relevant product. Thus, unverified data cannot only cost an intelligence product its Accuracy, but also damage its Relevance to the customer.[32]

Although Brei's principles do not require consumer input in the evaluation of intelligence, the process of measuring the effectiveness of a product is enhanced with consumer participation. Brei suggests: "[L]isten to their complaints."[33] However, this does not guarantee that the responses will address the product of interest. Rather, the analyst needs to ask directly for specific feedback from the consumer. This is most effective if the analysts and managers have collaborative relationships with consumers. Lacking such relationships, producers may attach survey questions to intelligence products, prompting consumers to respond regarding the utility of the service provided. Admittedly, this elicitation may be disturbing, as consumers are more likely to respond when they are unhappy with the product than when they are pleased. Further, regardless of the assessment of worth or value, some consumers will never respond.

Brei's principles provide a means for evaluating a given intelligence product based on the meaning it conveys and the value of that intelligence to the consumer. His approach, when combined with an "insider's" view of the intelligence production process, analytic methods and personnel management practices, makes a comprehensive evaluation of intelligence analysis appear possible. In the sections to follow, the concept of core competencies for intelligence analysis is developed, from which may emerge some useful suggestions for operationalizing the concept of an "art and science" of intelligence analysis.

---

[31] Brei, 6.

[32] Brei, 6.

[33] Brei, 5.

CHARACTERISTICS OF SUCCESSFUL INTELLIGENCE ANALYSTS

> A sophisticated intelligence analyst is one who is steeped in the history and culture of a region, has lifelong interest in the area, and approaches the study of the region as a professional responsibility, and probably as an avocation as well.
>
> — *Ronald D. Garst and Max L. Gross*[34]

Who are the most successful intelligence analysts? What makes them successful? In setting forth the functional core competencies for successful intelligence analysis we observe there are characteristics which, while not necessary for successful intelligence analysis per se, do seem to be associated with analysts considered to be the most successful at their trade.[35] It should be noted, however, that not all successful analysts exhibit all these characteristics. The characteristics highlighted in the graphic below are a representative superset, and while individual analysts do seem to share certain characteristics, they do not share all of them in equal measure.

Probably the most indispensable characteristics of successful intelligence analysts are high self-motivation and insatiable curiosity. Analysts want to know everything they can about the objects under their scrutiny. Reading and observing voraciously, they ferret out every possible piece of information and demonstrate a sense of wonder about what they discover. As new fragments appear, novel connections are discovered between the new and older information as a result of intense concentration leading to epiphanous moments of "aha" thinking. The most successful analysts tend to enjoy their work—"It's play, not work." Indeed, they often will stay late at the office to pursue a thorny problem or an engaging line of reasoning.

These characteristics also describe the values, standards, and beliefs of a dynamic, living analytic culture. As such, they may be used as preliminary indicators during the hiring process to identify prospective employees. A person with many of the characteristics listed may be predisposed to being a successful analyst, if the appropriate skills, abilities, and

---

[34] Ronald D. Garst and Max L. Gross, "On Becoming an Intelligence Analyst," *Defense Intelligence Journal* 6, no. 2 (Fall 1997): 55.

[35] The authors base their establishment of core competencies primarily on two initiatives taken as NSA in recent years. The first is an extensive formal job analysis conducted by industrial psychologists in the mid-1990s. Identification of some of the knowledge areas, skills and abilities required for intelligence analysis came out of that study, which is cited extensively in Lisa Krizan, *Intelligence Essentials for Everyone*, JMIC Occasional Paper Number Six (Washington, DC: JMIC, 1999). The second initiative is the ongoing work of the Arts and Science of Analysis research organization established at NSA in early 2000. As members of that organization, the authors participated in studies and interviews yielding insights into the behaviors applied by NSA intelligence analysts on the job.

necessary knowledge to perform the work are also present. Employee orientation programs that acknowledge these characteristics may be most successful in initiating new employees into the analytic culture. When personal characteristics are embodied in compelling "war stories" told by mentors and peers, they can reinforce the cultural values of the agency, building corporate loyalty by reinforcing the sense of membership.

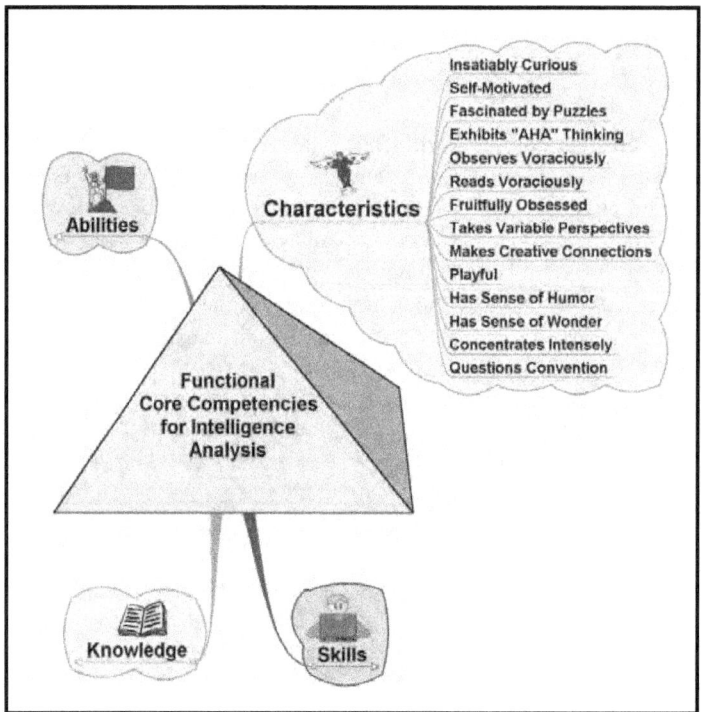

Characteristics of successful intelligence analysts.

Indoctrination into a particular analytic culture can also have negative implications. Although it may build loyalty, enhance behaviors, and inculcate values, it can also prevent objective analysis by reinforcing "group" thought patterns and analytic methodologies. The culture must allow for "a spirit of creativity to emerge and prosper."[36]

These personal characteristics of successful intelligence analysts are but one factor among many in influencing the success of intelligence process and product. Abilities and skills provide the tools for performing good intelligence analysis. Knowledge provides raw material for analysis as well as for an appreciation of the context and relevance of information.

---

[36] Don McDowell, *Strategic Intelligence: A Handbook for Practitioners, Managers, and Users* (Cooma, Australia: Istana Enterprises, Pty. Ltd., 1998), 216.

ABILITIES REQUIRED FOR INTELLIGENCE ANALYSIS

The competent intelligence analyst must have a unique combination of talents.
— *Ronald D. Garst and Max L. Gross*[37]

Abilities arise from aptitudes that can develop from an individual's innate, natural characteristics or talents. Although aptitudes may largely be determined by a person's genetic background, they may also be enhanced through training.[38] We find the abilities shown here to be necessary for intelligence analysis.

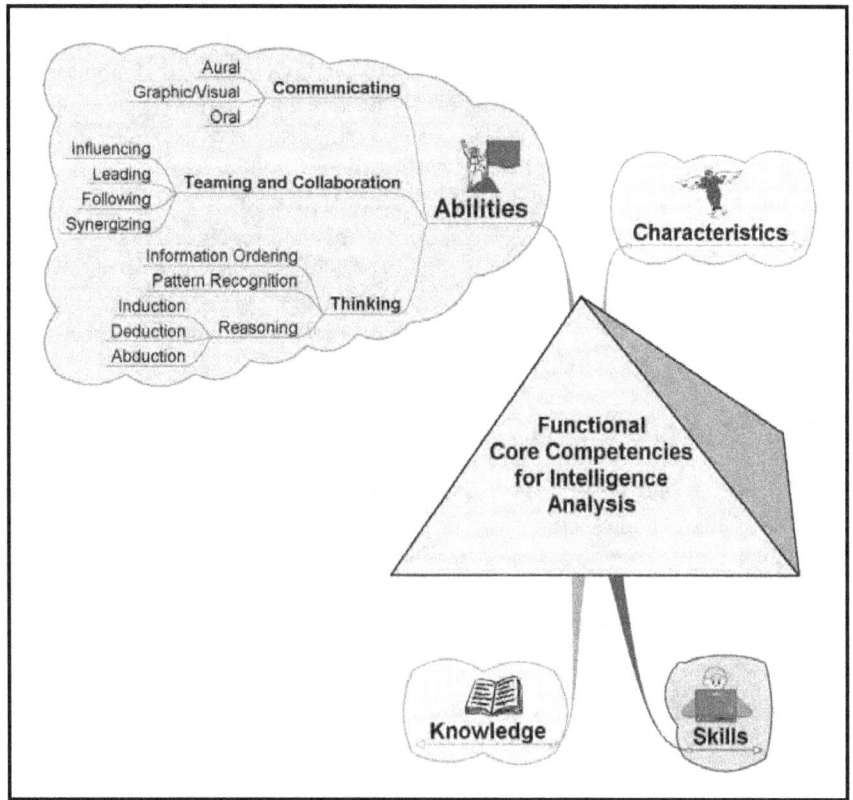

Abilities required for successful intelligence analysis.

---

[37]Garst and Gross, 47.

[38]Conversation with Dr. S. Alenka Brown-Vanhoozer, Director, Center for Cognitive Processing Technology, Advanced Computing Technologies, BWXT Y-12, Oak Ridge, TN, April 2001.

Communicating

Almost all animate life communicates, but humans are unique in possessing a brain structured to permit abstract, symbolic communication. Three communication abilities appear necessary for various aspects of intelligence analysis:[39]

■ **Aural:** The ability to hear, listen to, and understand spoken words and sentences is one of the essential means humans employ to take in information. Aural ability can be improved through specific techniques of "active listening." This ability greatly enhances analysts' performance of certain technical tasks, and their interaction with consumers, peers and managers.

■ **Graphic/Visual:** The ability to see, view, and understand graphic/visual symbols developed early in human history. Along with the ability to interpret symbols came the ability to present information in a graphic or visual manner so that others could understand. Even in speech, a majority of human communication remains non-verbal (that is, graphic or visual).[40] Developing this ability allows for effective graphical presentation of intelligence, which can dramatically heighten its impact.

■ **Oral:** The ability to communicate via spoken words and sentences so that others will understand is unique to humans. While the physical capability has evolved over eons, key developmental milestones occur during the first years of life. The development of oral and aural abilities are closely linked. Effective oral communication directly affects the intelligence analyst's credibility.

Teaming and Collaboration

Humans are a social species, and associated abilities have evolved with human development. Teaming and collaborating were essential when proto-humans moved from the relative safety of the trees onto the more dangerous plains of Africa. Their collective lives depended on social abilities to solve problems and overcome threats. While today's threats have changed, humans retain these abilities in order to live and work together.

Teaming and collaboration abilities enhance intelligence analysis, since the analyst's relationship with consumers, peers, subordinates, and supervisors shapes the intelligence production process. Formalized means of enhancing all these abilities can lead intelligence professionals to considerably greater effectiveness as analysts and leaders of analysts. This is why the Director of Central Intelligence has indicated that collaboration is a cornerstone of strategic intelligence.[41] A collaborative environment also minimizes the likelihood of intelligence failures. For example, had imagery analysts communicated

---

[39] We do not suggest that individuals lacking one or more of these abilities due to physical impairment would be unable to perform intelligence analysis. However, we do suggest that in the absence of corrective technologies, an impaired person may not be able to perform certain functions of analysis or production that depend on the impaired ability.

[40] Conversation with Dr. S. Alenka Brown-Vanhoozer, April 2001.

[41] Director of Central Intelligence National Security Advisory Panel, accessed 1 June 2001.

effectively with their counterpart area analysts in 1999, the "Yugoslav War Office" bombed by U.S. forces that spring may have been identified as the Chinese Embassy in time to avoid the resultant tragedy.[42]

We identify four distinct teaming abilities, to show the complexity of the concept. Typically, formal training programs address leadership abilities only in the context of the management function; here, we focus on the analysis process itself.

- **Influencing:** Those with this ability effectively and positively influence superiors, peers, and subordinates in intelligence work. Analysts often need to persuade others that their methods and conclusions are valid, and they often need to leverage additional resources. The ability to influence determines the level of success they will have in these areas.
- **Leading:** Those who are more senior, more skilled, and more successful in intelligence analysis have an obligation to lead, that is, to direct others and serve as role models. The ability to lead involves working with and through others to produce desired business outcomes. Thus, developing leadership abilities enhances the field of intelligence analysis.
- **Following:** Almost every grouping of humans has a leader. Everyone else is a follower. Analysts must enhance their abilities to work within a team, taking direction, and acting on it.
- **Synergizing:** Drawing on the other three teaming abilities, players in the intelligence process cooperate to achieve a common goal, the value of which is greater than they could achieve when working alone.

Thinking

> As our species designation—*sapiens*—suggests, the defining attribute of human beings is an unparalleled cognitive ability. We think differently from all other creatures on earth, and we can share those thoughts with one another in ways that no other species even approaches.
> — *Terence W. Deacon, The Symbolic Species.*[43]

Intelligence analysis is primarily a thinking process; it depends upon cognitive functions that evolved in humans long before the appearance of language.[44] The personal characteristics of intelligence analysts are manifested in behaviors that reflect thinking and/or the inherent drive to think. Our national survival may depend on having better developed thinking abilities than our opponents. Three basic thinking abilities are

---

[42] Gregory Treverton, 10.

[43] Terence W. Deacon, *The Symbolic Species: The Co-Evolution of Language and the Brain* (London: W.W. Norton & Company, Ltd., 1997), 21.

[44] Keith Devlin, "The Role of Conceptual Structure in Human Evolution" in Bernhard Ganter and Guy W. Mineau, eds, *Conceptual Structures: Logical, Linguistic, and Computational Issues*, 8th International Conference on Conceptual Structures (Berlin: Springier Verlag, 2000), 1.

required for intelligence analysis. Given the limitations imposed by each one of them, only simultaneous application of all three may yield successful intelligence analysis.

- **Information Ordering:** This ability involves following previously defined rules or sets of rules to arrange data in a meaningful order. In the context of intelligence analysis, this ability allows people, often with the assistance of technology, to arrange information in ways that permit analysis, synthesis, and extraction of meaning. The arrangement of information according to certain learned rules leads the analyst to make conclusions and disseminate them as intelligence. A danger arises, however, in that such ordering is inherently limiting—the analyst may not look for alternative explanations because the known rules lead to a ready conclusion.

- **Pattern Recognition:** Humans detect patterns and impose patterns on apparently random entities and events in order to understand them, often doing this without being aware of it. Stellar constellations are examples of imposed patterns, while criminal behavior analysis is an example of pattern detection. Intelligence analysts impose or detect patterns to identify what targets are doing, and thereby to extrapolate what they will do in the future. Pattern recognition lets analysts separate "the important from the less important, even the trivial, and to conceptualize a degree of order out of apparent chaos."[45] However, imposing or seeking patterns can introduce bias. Analysts may impose culturally defined patterns on random aggregates rather than recognize inherent patterns, thereby misinterpreting the phenomena in question.

- **Reasoning:** The ability to reason is what permits humans to process information and formulate explanations, to assign meaning to observed phenomena. It is by reasoning that analysts transform information into intelligence, in these three ways:

  1. **Induction:** Inductive reasoning combines separate fragments of information, or specific answers to problems, to form general rules or conclusions. For example, using induction, a child learns to associate the color red with heat and heat with pain, and then to generalize these associations to new situations.[46] Rigorous induction depends upon demonstrating the validity of causal relationships between observed phenomena, not merely associating them with each other.

  2. **Deduction:** Deductive reasoning applies general rules to specific problems to arrive at conclusions. Analysts begin with a set of rules and use them as a basis for interpreting information. For example, an analyst who follows the nuclear weapons program of a country might notice that a characteristic series of events preceded the last nuclear weapons test. Upon seeing evidence that those same events are occurring again, the analyst might deduce that a second nuclear test is imminent.[47] However, this conclusion would be made cautiously, since deduction works best in

---

[45] Garst and Gross, 47.

[46] Jerome K. Clauser and Sandra M. Weir, *Intelligence Research Methodologies, An Introduction to Techniques and Procedures for Conducting Research in Defense Intelligence* (Washington DC: Defense Intelligence School, 1975), 81.

[47] Clauser and Weir, 81.

closed systems such as mathematics, making it of limited use in forecasting human behavior.

3. **Abduction:** Abductive reasoning describes the thought process that accompanies "insight" or intuition. When the information does not match that expected, the analyst asks "why?," thereby generating novel hypotheses to explain given evidence that does not readily suggest a familiar explanation. For example, given two shipping manifests, one showing oranges and lemons being shipped from Venezuela to Florida, and the other showing carnations being shipped from Delaware to Colombia, abductive reasoning is what enables the analyst to take an analytic leap and ask, "Why is citrus fruit being sent to the worldwide capital of citrus farming, while carnations are being sent to the world's primary exporter of that product? What is really going on here?" Thus, abduction relies on the analyst's preparation and experience to suggest possible explanations that must then be tested. Abduction generates new research questions rather than solutions.[48]

---

[48] Chong Ho Yu, "Abduction? Deduction? Induction? Is There a Logic of Exploratory Data Analysis," Paper presented at the annual meeting of the American Education Research Association, New Orleans, LA, April 1994, URL: *http://seamonkey.ed.asu.edu/~behrens/asu/reports/Peirce/Logic_of_EDA.html*, accessed 6 June 2001.

SKILLS REQUIRED FOR INTELLIGENCE ANALYSIS

Any institution that relies on professionals for success and seeks to maintain an authentic learning climate for individual growth must require its members to read (to gain knowledge and insight), research (to learn how to ask good questions and find defensible answers), discuss (to appreciate opposing views and subject their own to rigorous debate), and write (to structure arguments and articulate them clearly and coherently).

— Gregory D. Foster[49]

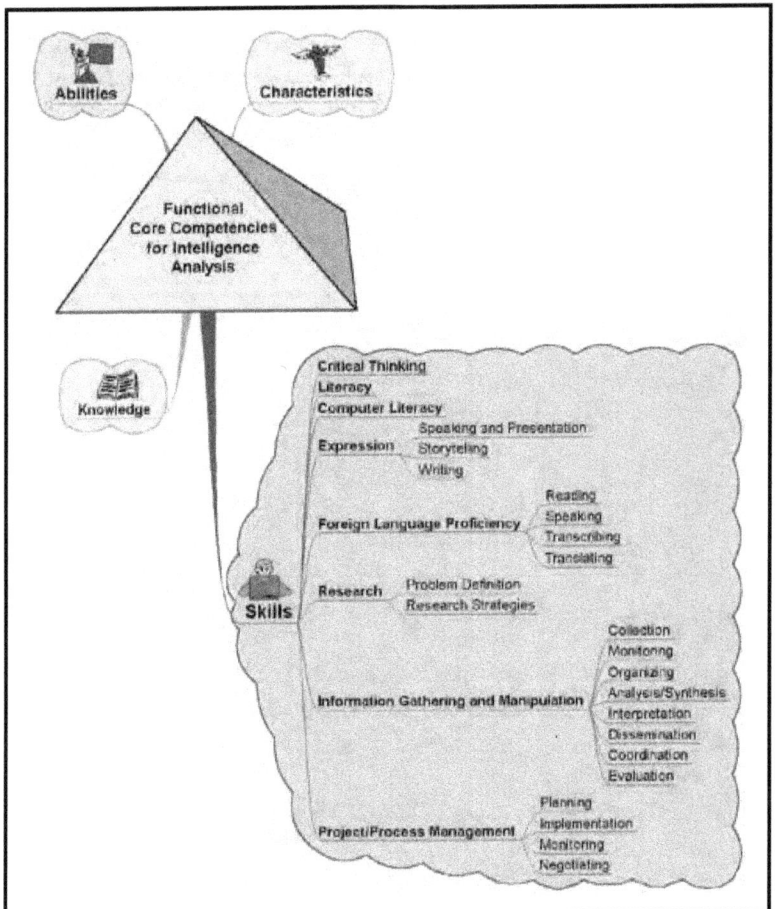

Skills required for successful intelligence analysis.

---

[49] Gregory D. Foster, "Research, Writing, and the Mind of the Strategist," *Joint Force Quarterly* 11 (Spring 1996): 74-79.

Whereas aptitudes and related abilities probably stem from an analyst's genetic makeup, a skill represents learned expertise or proficiency based on a particular ability or set of abilities. At least eight types of skills, shown here, are required for successful intelligence analysis.

Critical Thinking

It is by thinking that analysts transform information into intelligence. Critical thinking is the cognitive skill applied to make that transformation. Critical thinking can be defined as

> [An] intellectually disciplined process of actively and skillfully conceptualizing, applying, analyzing, synthesizing, and/or evaluating information gathered from, or generated by, observation, experience, reflection, reasoning, or communication, as a guide to belief and action....Thinking about [our] thinking while [we're] thinking in order to make [our] thinking better.[50]

> There is a clear need to educate and train intelligence analysts to use their minds...[Only] by raising their awareness can the intelligence unit be assured that the analysts will avoid the traps in being slave to conformist thought, precedent and imposed cultural values—all enemies of objective analysis.[51]

An ordered thinking process requires careful judgments or judicious evaluations leading to defensible conclusions that provide an audit trail. When the results of analysis are controversial, subject to alternate interpretations, or possibly wrong, this audit trail can prove essential in defending the process used to reach the conclusions.

Effective critical thinking also includes routine, systematic questioning of the premises upon which decisions are based. Without critical thinking, current beliefs and methods are not questioned, as long as they appear to produce results that can be reasonably explained. Yet they can prevent analysts from making alternative interpretations. Writing rhetorically, Gregory Treverton asks, "If intelligence doesn't challenge prevailing mind-sets, what good is it?"[52]

Intelligence failure can be the result when alternative premises are ignored, as happened from the mid-1970s to the mid-1990s in Sweden. During that time, the Swedish Navy expended considerable effort and ordnance attempting to "destroy" intruding Soviet submarines. Swedish naval analysts (and others) repeatedly acknowledged failure, rationalizing it as a "David versus Goliath" contest: Sweden's tiny navy was no match for the

---

[50] National Drug Intelligence Center, *Basic Intelligence Analysis Course*, # 9, PowerPoint Presentation, April 2001.

[51] McDowell, 216.

[52] Treverton, 5.

technologically advanced Soviet submarine fleet. It was not until 1995 that Swedish defense chief Owe Wiktorin revealed the truth; detected intruders previously believed to be submarines were in fact minks swimming in the waters off the Swedish coast. Blinded by the premise that the Soviets wanted to make war against Sweden, the navy had ignored this possible explanation for their failure to destroy "enemy" submarines, despite the fact that the alternative premise had been suggested as early as 1987.[53] An obvious conclusion from this story is that corporate mechanisms for questioning analytic premises could have resolved this intelligence question nearly a decade earlier. The lesson for present-day intelligence analysts is clear: corporate processes for intelligence analysis must allow for, and indeed, institutionalize, the questioning of premises.

Literacy

Intelligence analysis requires the reading and comprehension of written sentences and paragraphs, often in multiple languages, at many points in the intelligence process. Prospective intelligence analysts must be literate in order to perform their work at the most basic level, making this skill a prerequisite for employment. Literacy skills are crucial for understanding the target, the consumer and the intelligence process. Literacy is also necessary for conducting research.

Computer Literacy

It is a given that in the 21st Century, the computer is an essential tool for intelligence analysis. Today, analysts must be highly skilled in the use of computers themselves and in the use of software that will aid analysis. Word processing, spreadsheet, and presentation programs, as well as specific programs that assist at all stages of the analytic process, are the essential tools that can bolster success. However, tools themselves do not provide "truth" (if such can be said to exist in the intelligence analysis context). Rather, these tools for manipulation, correlation, and presentation of information are a means to an end: the production of intelligence. An analyst's skillful use of them hastens arrival at that end.

The fact that analysts are faced with massive volumes of data also makes use of selection and filtering tools essential. The analyst depends on these tools to make a "first cut" on the collected information. The tools are used to filter non-relevant information items and retain only those items that are pertinent to the issue being analyzed.

Expression

The results of analysis are useless if they are poorly presented. "The capable analyst must be competent and experienced in presenting analysis both orally and in writing."[54] Effective oral and written skills are therefore essential for the intelligence analyst. Fail-

---

[53] William H. Starbuck, "Unlearning Ineffective or Obsolete Technologies," *International Journal of Technology Management* 11, nos. 7/8 (Winter 1996): 725-726.

[54] Garst and Gross, 49.

ures of intelligence can indeed occur when the results of analysis are inadequately presented. For example, Berkowitz and Goodman note that lengthy daily or weekly briefings may be inadequate means for informing officials, regardless of their content. Warnings go "unheard because the officials [find] the hour-long briefings to be an inefficient use of their time and [stop] attending."[55] Similarly, they conclude that inadequate intelligence reporting of unrest in Iran in 1978 contributed to the U.S. Intelligence Community's failure to predict the fall of the Shah.[56] These examples also make it clear that whichever method of informing policymakers is selected, the resultant products must be concise, tailored ones that masterfully present the intelligence to the intended consumer or in the consumer's frame of reference.

- **Speaking and Presentation:** The oral presentation of information, particularly to senior officials, otherwise known as "briefing," and often accompanied by visual aids, allows an effective analyst to tailor both the content and delivery method to the consumer's abilities or predilections. The briefing's timing, level of detail, format and tone may all be matched to the consumer. In particular, key facts and conclusions come at the beginning of the exchange and determine its organization.[57] Effective briefing goes beyond these technical considerations. The heart of the intelligence briefing is the presenter's relationship with the consumer, thus, "the essence of briefing is not simply the projection of information, but rather the art of promoting understanding between individuals."[58] Through the briefing process, the presenter puts information into the consumer's frame of reference, making clear the possibilities for decision, action and consequences, thereby creating intelligence.

- **Storytelling:** While well-honed speaking and presentation skills allow effective intelligence dissemination, well developed storytelling skills ensure that intelligence is convincingly conveyed. Storytelling involves more than just creating the story. Its power lies in the way the story is told. In the words of transformational storytelling expert Stephen Denning, "[the] look of the eye, the intonation of the voice, the way the body is held, the import of a subtle pause, and [the storyteller's] own response to the audience's responses—all these aspects ... make an immense contribution to the meaning of the story for [the] audience."[59] Too often the consumer does not understand a poorly told but important story buried in a sophisticated presentation, making storytelling an essential skill for intelligence professionals.

---

[55] Bruce D. Berkowitz and Allan E. Goodman, *Strategic Intelligence for American National Security* (Princeton: Princeton University Press, 1989), 32.

[56] Berkowitz and Goodman, 202.

[57] Krizan, 40, 42-46.

[58] Benjamin T. Buring, LT, USN, *Function vs. Form: Successfully Briefing the Intelligence Story*, MSSI thesis (Washington, DC: JMIC, August 2001), 24.

[59] Stephen Denning, *The Springboard: How Storytelling Ignites Action in Knowledge-Era Organizations* (Boston, MA: Butterworth Heineman, 2001), xxii.

Storytelling in this context is not about fiction; it is not about "once upon a time." Rather, intelligence storytelling involves creating scenarios and alternative futures for consumers. Intelligence assessments that provide a variety of possible outcomes, recounted in considerable detail, can give the consumer clues to the most effective policies or strategies. An example of varying analytic outcomes expressed as scenarios can be found in the National Intelligence Council's *Global Trends 2015*. Four alternative futures for the next 15 years are outlined in addition to the principal scenario. These alternatives suggest a variety of possible outcomes based on population trends, resource availability, technological advances, economic conditions, ethnic identity and governance, and local and regional conflicts. The significance for the policymaker is that the future is fluid.[60] While all the alternatives are possible, certain political and strategic decisions could influence which outcome is most likely to occur. Being prepared for various outcomes enables the policymaker to be proactive and to respond appropriately as events unfold.

- **Writing:** The basic vehicle by which intelligence historically has been purveyed is the written report. At the beginning of the 21st Century this remains the case. Yet many contemporary intelligence analysts lack this basic skill, and improvement "of writing skills, basic though it may be, is often required as part of becoming a competent intelligence analyst."[61]

Foreign Language Proficiency

To be truly successful, analysts must be proficient in the language(s) employed by the subjects of their analysis. Without such proficiency they cannot completely comprehend target intentions and actions. When analysts misunderstand their targets, the intelligence they provide to consumers thus will be inaccurate or misleading.

Once upon a time, many intelligence analysts could rely upon the skills of professional linguists for translation of target information. Now this luxury has become unavailable to all but a few intelligence analysts working the largest, best-funded intelligence problems.[62] Foreign language proficiency has thus become a necessity for all who perform intelligence analysis.

If budget and personnel cuts are insufficient reason for analysts to have foreign language proficiency, changes in intelligence targets provide additional arguments for its necessity. Although targets of interest have traditionally used their native language(s) for internal communications, many employed non-native languages such as English for international communications and publications. This was especially true of the first decade of

---

[60] National Intelligence Council, 2000, 83-85.

[61] Berkowitz and Goodman, 54.

[62] For one view of the staffing cuts at the National Security Agency, see Mathew M. Aid, "The Time of Troubles: The US National Security Agency in the Twenty-First Century," *Intelligence and National Security* 15, no. 3, (Autumn 2000): 5-9.

the popular use of the Internet, when English was the *lingua franca* of that medium. However, this is changing. The use of native languages in international communications is growing both on and off the Internet. Thus, proficiency in non-English languages is necessary for analysis of information, approximately 80 percent of which "is *not* secret, is *not* online, is *not* in English, is *not* government associated, but is in the private sector, and is *not* available locally to the analyst."[63]

Furthermore, foreign language proficiency provides more than just a translation of non-English materials. The structure of a target's language and that target's culture are closely related. One well-known theory of this relationship, by Edward Sapir and Benjamin Whorf, posits that "language is a force in its own right and it affects how individuals in a society conceive and perceive reality."[64] Thus concepts essential to understanding the target are communicated in a context that goes beyond simplistic translation.

For example, the German terms *Gemeinschaft* and *Gesellschaft* both translate into English as "community." Yet this translation ignores the interpersonal nature of the relationship among the members of the first type of community, and the business context of the second. An analyst relying on translation by another might not be aware of the nature of the "community" in the material being analyzed.

In Somali there are two pronouns for the English "we." A speaker of Somali uses the pronoun *annagu* when referring to the speaker and someone other than the person being addressed. Conversely, the use of the pronoun *innagu* includes the person being addressed. So if someone says in English, "We are going to the movie," the question of "Who is 'we'?" must be asked. In Somali there is no doubt: If annagu are going to the movies, the person being addressed is not going; if innagu are going to the movies then the person being addressed is going. Again, an analyst depending on a translation into English must rely on the translator to convey that contextual information. This inclusion or exclusion from a group can be quite significant. There is a considerable difference between "annagu are going to blow up the embassy," and "innagu are going to blow up the embassy." This distinction is especially significant to the intelligence analyst in this case, even if the implications for the embassy remain the same.

Even the distinction between intelligence and information is language-derived. The Sinitic term *qingbao* refers to a concept that can be understood either as "information" or "intelligence."[65] This latter distinction is a "Western one not shared by East Asian languages or presumably their speakers," according to the Foreign Broadcast Information

---

[63]Robert David Steele, "The New Craft of Intelligence: an Alternative Approach Oriented to the Public," Conference on The Future of Intelligence in the 21st Century, Priverno, Italy, 14-16 February 2001. The quote is from Steele's remarks and is not in his published version of the paper. Clarification was made via personal email communication, 18 May 2001. Because the conference operated under the "Chatham House Rule," Mr. Steele is quoted with permission.

[64]Carol R. Ember and Melvin Ember, *Anthropology*, 9th ed. (Upper Saddle River: Prentice Hall, 1999), 225.

[65]*Concise English-Chinese/Chinese-English Dictionary*, 2nd ed. (Oxford: Oxford University Press, 1999), 363.

Service editor of the Chinese intelligence collection manual, *Guofang Keji Qingbaoyuan ji Houqu Jishu*.[66] Context must determine the translation, and an analyst lacking foreign language skills must trust the linguist to correctly understand that context. The expertise required for that understanding might render the linguist a better intelligence analyst than the original analyst. This begs the question: "Is such duplication of personnel affordable?"

We recognize that certain forms of technical analysis have previously not required foreign language proficiency. We suggest, however, that it is not truly known, nor can we know, whether foreign language proficiency would have enhanced that analysis. Some technical metadata analysis clearly does not require language proficiency. However, analysis of other types of metadata may indeed require foreign language proficiency and we caution against dismissing out of hand the need for it. Furthermore, staffing cuts require that analysts review both data and metadata. Even if the metadata do not require foreign language competency, the underlying data do require it. In addition, essential technical meaning is lost in the translation between linguist and technical analyst; technical analysts often need that original source and its context. This can be gained only from proficiency in the original language. Ultimately, foreign language proficiency enables the analyst to engage in a holistic, comprehensive analytic process.

We see a connection between the depth at which the analyst must work a target and the degree of required foreign language proficiency. If analysts work a great many targets at a superficial level, they need only have a casual acquaintance with their language(s). Similarly, when analysts are assigned to an *ad hoc* crisis cell working a specific target for a finite period, they may also need only superficial language skills. In this latter case, if the crisis is of sufficient importance, dedicated language assets will be assigned to compensate for their ignorance. However, should the crisis become long-term, it is reasonable to expect them to acquire more than a passing skill in the target's language(s).

Research

Research skills provide discipline and consistency for the creation of value-added intelligence. By providing methodologies for defining the requirement to be answered, as well as methodologies for answering that query, research skills ensure analytic consistency and enable thorough exploration of the issues. Necessary research skills include methods of problem definition that ensure that, in collaboration with the consumer, analysts correctly define or redefine the problem in terms of a "research question," so as to understand the consumer's and the analyst's own objectives.[67] Research strategies, when based on the issue to be answered, help identify required sources of information, the means of information collection, and the means of analyzing and synthesizing the data.

---

[66] FBIS Editor's comments on the English translation of Huo, Zhongwen and Wang, Zongxiao, Guofang Keji Qingbaoyuan ji Houqu Jishu (Sources and Techniques of Obtaining National Defense Science and Technology Intelligence) (Beijing: Kexue Jishu Wenxuan Publishing Co., 1991).

[67] Russell G. Swenson and others, "Research Design," in *Research: Design and Methods* (Washington DC: Joint Military Intelligence College, 2001), 19-20. This publication is an essential guide for Community analysts developing research and analytic strategies for long-term projects.

Information Gathering and Manipulation

Information is the grist for intelligence analysis, and to be successful, analysts must aggressively seek it out. Different information/data manipulation skills are required for the various stages of the intelligence process.

- **Collection:** This stage involves gathering information from all sources. The intelligence analyst directs the collection process, causing specific resources to be tasked. Related information manipulation skills include selecting and filtering in order to assess whether the information and its sources are of value.

- **Monitoring:.** Reliability of sources and the validity of the information are always in question. Monitoring skills focus on information review, and often may involve analysis of descriptors and summaries of that data.

- **Organizing:** Skillful arrangement, formatting, and maintenance of data for analysis and technical report generation ensure access to materials in a usable format.

- **Analysis/Synthesis:** Information manipulation skills can point to patterns, relationships, anomalies and trends.

- **Interpretation:** This is the stage in the process where information is transformed into intelligence by cognitive manipulation, that is, assigning meaning to analyzed and synthesized information using critical thinking. Computers aid in this step, however, a study of 12 major "analytic" software tools concludes "true analysis will remain a people function, assisted by computer technology."[68]

- **Dissemination:** Dissemination, except for some graphic products, is now of course mostly electronic. Information preparation and presentation skills allow its transformation and publication, so that the results of analysis appear in usable formats, which may be further tailored by users.

- **Coordination:** Coordination requires analysts as well as their managers to employ "collegial" skills in the bureaucratic environment; these skills are also needed to avoid diluting the intelligence message down to the "lowest common level of agreement."

- **Evaluation:** Internal and intra-community evaluation allows the intelligence to be discussed and placed in larger contexts than that viewed by a single agency. Such collaboration may also identify the additional intelligence required to clarify issues. Evaluation can become a continuous part of the production process.[69]

Project/Process Management

Few analysts enjoy the luxury of working full time on only one problem or on one aspect of a particular problem. We distinguish between projects and processes. The former tend to have finite scope and goals whereas the latter are open-ended. Both require planning, imple-

---

[68] Leonard Fuld, Fuld Associates, "Intelligence Software: Reality or Still Virtual Reality," *Competitive Intelligence Magazine* 4, no. 2 (March-April, 2001): 24-25.

[69] See also Brei.

mentation, monitoring, and negotiating skills.[70] A project/process plan defines and clarifies what needs to be accomplished; identifies necessary resources; creates a timeline, including milestones; and makes the analyst accountable for successful completion.

KNOWLEDGE REQUIRED FOR INTELLIGENCE ANALYSIS

Without a solid knowledge base concerning the region or issue to which the analyst is assigned, . . . the individual will not even know what questions to ask. That is, the person will not really be qualified to be called an "analyst."
— *Ronald D. Garst and Max L. Gross*[71]

Knowledge consists of familiarities, awareness, or understanding gained through experience or study; it includes both empirical material and that derived by inference or interpretation.[72] Depending on the specific target, the knowledge required can vary widely. Our essential subset is shown in the figure and discussed below.

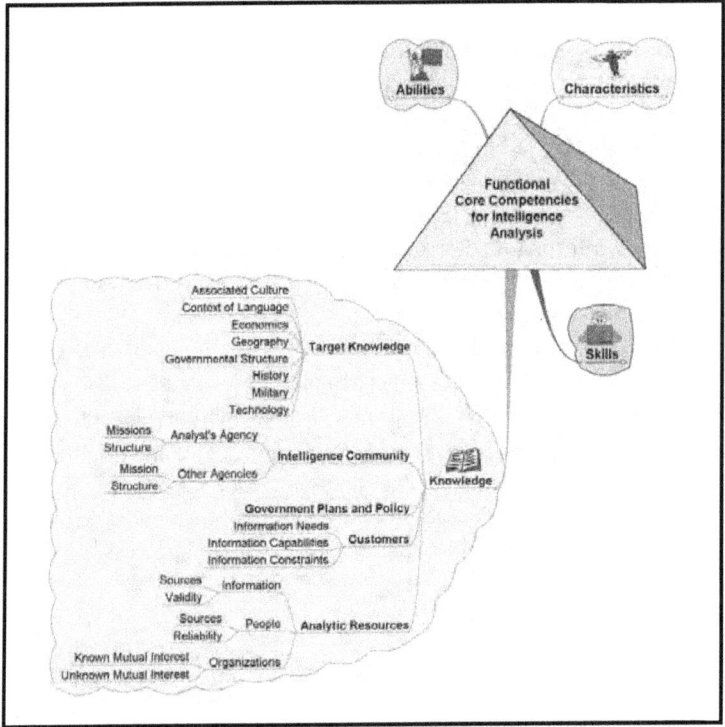

Knowledge required for successful intelligence analysis.

[70] Clifford C. Kalb, "Core Competencies: A Practitioner's View," document 207612, Merck & Co., Inc, n.d.

[71] Garst and Gross, 50.

Target Knowledge

Doing intelligence analysis in the information age is often like "being driven by someone with tunnel vision."[73] In the quest to answer a consumer's questions, the analyst often pushes aside "all the fuzzy stuff that lies around the edge—context, background, history, common knowledge, social resources."[74] Yet, to do so is perilous, for these provide balance and perspective. They offer breadth of vision and ultimately allow analysts to make sense of the information under study. By providing the context into which analysts place their work, fields of study such as anthropology, comparative religion, economics, geography, history, international relations, psychology, and sociology all interact to contribute vital knowledge about the target, which both analysts and consumers need to understand. Changes in the culture, religion, geography, or economic systems (among others) of a target may themselves be subjects of an intelligence requirement.

Gregory Treverton asserts that intelligence "is supposed to have the people who understand Bonn and Delhi better than they do Washington."[75] Without such understanding, intelligence and policy failures can occur. Treverton blames the failure of the U.S. Intelligence Community to predict India's 1998 nuclear test partially on a lack of understanding by U.S. analysts of "true" Indian motivations. He asserts that a questioning of premises coupled with greater knowledge of the reasons why India would want to conduct a nuclear test should have led U.S. analysts to different conclusions.[76]

The following selection of topics exemplifies some non-traditional but essential target knowledge areas required for thorough intelligence analysis.

- **Culture:** Culture can be defined as a group's values, standards, and beliefs. In turn, culture defines that group. The study of culture reveals the roles of individuals in the community, and how they relate to non-members of the culture. This provides insights into behaviors that are of value in predicting future behavior. This is true when the target is a people or a nation as well as when the target is a specific subgroup or individual member within a culture. Adda Bozeman points out that because political systems are grounded in cultures, "present day international relations are therefore by definition also intercultural relations ... [A]nalysts and policymakers in the West would be more successful in their respective callings if they would examine the cultural infrastructures of the nations and political systems they are dealing with."[77]
- **Message of Language:** The message of language is a part of culture, and while isolating it makes an artificial distinction, we do so to reiterate its importance for intelli-

---

[72] Knowledge," *The American Heritage Dictionary*, 2nd College Edition, 1976 Ed.

[73] John Seely Brown and Paul Duguid, *The Social Life of Information* (Boston: Harvard Business School Press, 2000), 1-2.

[74] Garst and Gross, 49.

[75] Treverton, 5.

[76] Treverton, 5.

[77] Adda Bozeman, *Politics and Culture in International History: From the Ancient Near East to the Opening of the Modern Age*, 2nd ed. (New Brunswick, NJ: Transaction Publishers, 1994), 5.

gence analysis. What languages are utilized, by whom, and in what context, is essential in understanding the target's culture. For example, much is revealed if members of an insurgent group primarily communicate using the language of the elite members of their culture. Additionally, what the language indicates about class and personal relationships may provide clues to behaviors.

- **Technology:** Technology itself can be the subject of study by the intelligence analyst. Someone developing a target may analyze specific technologies and their infrastructure as they pertain to that target. Further, the role of technology within a region, nation, or people is an indicator of behavior. The domains of communications, utilities, transportation, manufacturing, and others, as well as the attitudes of the people to them, are rich sources of study. Technology also can provide insights into sources of information that will be available to the intelligence analyst.

Professional Knowledge

In addition to understanding their targets, intelligence analysts need to know a great deal about the context and nature of the intelligence profession, and the resources available to help them do their job well. Understanding the plans and policies of their own government enables analysts to frame their work in terms of the nation's strategic and tactical objectives. Intelligence consumers are government officials. Their needs drive analytical process and priorities. Analysts base collection tasking on the imperative to match information sources to consumer needs. These information sources, such as human-source reporting, signals intercepts and documentary research, provide the analyst with raw materials for the creation of intelligence through analysis, synthesis and interpretation.

Determining what information must be analyzed is a precursor to the analytic process. Berkowitz and Goodman identify "four different types of 'information' [used by intelligence analysts] in preparing reports and estimates: known facts, secrets, disinformation, and mysteries."[78] Known facts and secrets must be placed in context or "revealed," disinformation must be discounted, and consumers must be informed that mysteries cannot be answered. For this to occur, the types of information available and their validity, as well as the sources of that information and their reliability, must be determined.

In addition, analysts need to know what specific sources of information relevant to a particular inquiry are available for exploitation. Knowing which expert sources and subject matter experts can guide the analytic process, or can offer different or additional perspectives, enhances intelligence work. The reliability of these sources is also critical. When different sources provide contradictory information, the reliability of one source versus another may provide insights into which information is accurate; the sources may be open or secret, technical or human.

Finally, others, known and unknown, may be examining similar information for the same or different consumers. Awareness that sources of information, possibly vital infor-

---

[78] Berkowitz and Goodman, 86.

mation, exist, even though they remain undiscovered or untapped, keeps the analyst constantly seeking out new connections.

IMPLICATIONS FOR THE INTELLIGENCE ANALYSIS WORKFORCE

Returning to our thesis, what makes an intelligence analyst successful? Given that the analyst's purpose is to create intelligence, success means following an effective process (rigorous analysis, sound management) and creating a quality product (that conveys intelligence and meets the consumer's needs). To do this requires appropriate abilities, knowledge and personal characteristics for rigorous intelligence analysis and production. Well-honed capabilities to communicate, cooperate and think, coupled with the skills that ensure technical competency, provide the means for intelligence work. Informed, deep knowledge of the issues and their background provides both content and context for analysis. Analysts who are motivated to succeed, to know targets, and to share that knowledge ensure that consumers receive intelligence of the highest caliber.

But do intelligence analysts today approach this ideal? And can we find or grow such talent to serve the Community's mission well into the 21st century?

> Of all the personnel problems the intelligence community will face in the coming years, the most difficult to solve is likely to be maintaining the base of talent the community requires to carry out its mission.... [Much] of the work of the intelligence community is highly specialized and requires exceptional creativity.... It is also safe to say that some of the most pressing analytic skills the community will require are precisely those we cannot even foresee at this time.
> — *Bruce D. Berkowitz and Allan E. Goodman*[79]

Berkowitz and Goodman's judgment from 1989 remains true in 2002. The Intelligence Community remains significantly challenged to maintain and enhance an analytic talent base against numerous rapidly changing threats to national security. Further, a possible uptick in hiring and rising rates of eligibility for retirement mean that, at the least, the savvy of the analytic population will continue to dwindle at the lower end and retire from the upper end.[80] Even an adequately sized analytic workforce, lacking adequate mentoring and training from senior, expert analysts, will leave the Intelligence Community unable to meet security challenges. For example, while NSA's technological capability remains widely recognized, former director General Kenneth A. Minihan noted, "If we

---

[79] Berkowitz and Goodman, 154.

[80] External Team Report: A management Review for the Director, NSA, 22 October 1999, URL: <http://www.nsa.gov/releases/nsa_external_team_report.pdf>, accessed 4 June 2001. For a different but related perspective see also the report of the "internal" New Enterprise Team, URL: *http://www.nsa.gov/releases/nsa_new_enterprise_team_recommendations.pdf*.

don't win the talent war, it doesn't matter if we invest in the infrastructure."[81]   According to the Council on Foreign Relations' independent report on the future of intelligence, "less than a tenth of what the United States spends on intelligence is devoted to analysis; it is the least expensive dimension of intelligence....This country could surely afford to spend more in those areas of analysis where being wrong can have major adverse consequences."[82] Winning the talent war requires smart investment in the hiring, training, and deployment of analysts.

With simultaneous greening and greying of the analytic workforce, analysts as a group may lack many of the core competencies necessary for successful intelligence analysis. A strategic requirement exists to resolve this problem. However, the authors know of no stratagem under consideration other than their own focus on identifying core competencies for management attention. It may be feasible to conduct small-scale, *ad hoc* or more systematic experimentation with specific analytic techniques such as that pioneered by Folker, to determine which techniques may hold the most promise for improved rigor of analysis.[83] We suspect that some experienced analysts do already match the ideal described above, although others are still operating within the outdated Cold War paradigm. Further, many novice analysts also have the willingness and potential to develop toward the ideal. But they need tradecraft mentors and teachers. Presently, there are not enough expert analysts to do both the teaching and the performance of sophisticated intelligence production.

Therefore, the Intelligence Community needs ways to enable intelligence analysts now on the job to enhance their professional skills. One approach to this problem is to provide widespread, specialized training in analytic methods. In order, however, to ensure that subsequently produced intelligence is accurate and useful, such training must focus on rigorous analytic processes that minimize biases introduced by the analyst, the consumer, the sources of the information, or the information itself. Collaborative training efforts such as those proposed in the *Strategic Investment Plan for Intelligence Community Analysis* offer another way by which intelligence analysts can acquire the skills necessary to bring greater rigor to their analyses.[84]

One analytic method in particular, known as "Analysis of Competing Hypotheses," as presented by Central Intelligence Agency (CIA) analyst Richards J. Heuer, Jr., provides a readily applicable approach to rigorous intelligence analysis. In Heuer's methodology, as used at the CIA, the analyst begins with a full set of alternative possibilities rather than the apparent single most likely alternative. Then the analyst compares each piece of evidence against each hypothesis, and determines if that evidence supports or refutes it. Evi-

---

[81] Quoted in Robert K. Ackerman, "Security Agency Transitions from Backer to Participant," Signal 54, no. 2 (October 1999): 23.

[82] Council on Foreign Relations, 1996, 11-12.

[83] Folker, *Intelligence Analysis in Theater Joint Intelligence Centers: An Experiment in Applying Structured Methods.*

[84] Director of Central Intelligence National Security Advisory Panel, 29ff.

dence that has no diagnostic value is taken out of consideration. After noting the evidence chain attached to each hypothesis, the analyst selects as the most probable hypothesis the one with the least amount of evidence against it. This contrasts with conventional analysis, which generally entails looking for evidence to confirm a favored hypothesis. Following the scientific method, Analysis of Competing Hypotheses seeks to eliminate hypotheses, whereas conventional analysis seeks to prove them.[85] The end result of the former is an actionable intelligence product that adds value to the consumer's development and execution of policy or strategy.

Folker's recent experiments in Theater Joint Intelligence Centers provide enticing evidence that such rigorous methods do foster analytic excellence. In four experiments, Folker provided analysts with one hour of training in Analysis of Competing Hypotheses, and then presented them with two realistic scenarios requiring analytic judgments and conclusions. A significantly greater number of the newly trained analysts derived the correct answers to the scenarios than analysts in a control group that used their own *ad hoc* methods. These findings demonstrate that while "exploiting a structured methodology cannot guarantee a correct answer, using a structured methodology ensures that analysis is performed and not overlooked." [86]

Folker therefore recommends widespread teaching of these methodologies during "both initial and subsequent training."[87] However, training is of little value unless it can be immediately applied. Thus organizational structures, culture, and processes must be aligned to permit and to reward rigorous analysis. Unless analysts are recognized and appreciated for performing sophisticated analysis, they will not embrace change. Significant recognition for high-level analysis will inspire others to follow, creating a culture that fosters and sustains excellence in tailored intelligence production.

Even if the entire analytic workforce were to adopt rigorous analytic techniques, the Intelligence Community may still lack sufficient resources to meet consumer needs. It will still need to hire new analysts, either from outside the agency or from within. However, these new employees must be highly qualified. The government cannot afford remedial training for prospective new employees lacking the necessary abilities and skills for intelligence analysis. Similarly, employees transferring into the analytic disciplines from other fields must have the prerequisite abilities and skills for analysis before joining this discipline. The field of intelligence analysis cannot safely be a catchall for employees transferring from downsized career fields.

---

[85] For a discussion of the Analysis of Competing Hypotheses see Chapter 8 of Richards J. Heuer, Jr., *The Psychology of Intelligence Analysis* (Washington, DC: Center for the Study of Intelligence, 1999).

[86] Folker, 33.

[87] Folker, 33.

Some prospective new hires do come to the discipline with an academic background in intelligence, and many current employees pursue continuing studies related to intelligence. However, intelligence studies at the university level tend to focus on intelligence and policy, not on tradecraft. Further, it is questionable whether the fledgling field of intelligence studies by itself yet offers the wherewithal to support a claim of expertise by someone educated in that specialty, except in the narrow, self-assessed areas of intelligence process or organization. Only one non-governmental institution in the U.S. offers an undergraduate degree in intelligence research and analysis: Mercyhurst College in Pennsylvania; there, too, advanced studies are offered in conjunction with a law-enforcement related degree. Within several years, the University of New Mexico expects to offer undergraduate through doctoral degrees in intelligence; the stated goals of this program are to focus on the tradecraft of strategic intelligence.[88] Other institutions, such as Wright State University in Ohio, are beginning intelligence analysis programs. But these academic programs are too small and too limited to meet the needs of government intelligence agencies for qualified analysts.

Furthermore, general academic preparation is not enough. Training new and current intelligence analysts in professional tradecraft is a Community responsibility and obligation. Analysts need both specific job-related training and enculturation appropriate to their agencies' missions. With the investment of adequate resources, including the development of modern curricula in intelligence tradecraft, Community training programs can meet these specialized analytic training needs. This investment also can include partnering with academic institutions offering "distance learning" programs and other means of outsourcing instructional resources.

The Aspin-Brown Commission on the Roles and Capabilities of the United States Intelligence Community identified several additional actions to improve the quality of analysis. These include a minimal prerequisite to visit target countries as part of analytic orientation, rewards for acquiring and maintaining foreign language proficiency, encouragement to remain within substantive areas of expertise, and periodic rotational assignments to consumer agencies.[89] Enacted as part of employee training and orientation, these measures can substantially enhance analysts' target knowledge and skills.

In combination with the right knowledge, skills, abilities, characteristics, and methodologies, the organizational and structural changes under consideration offer a possibility to genuinely transform the analytic work force. Specific changes in analytic culture, processes, and techniques offer the Intelligence Community a unique opportunity to rebuild analysis to effectively cope with a changed world. The recognition that technol-

---

[88] James Hold en-Rhodes, personal communications, 11-14 June 2001.

[89] Aspin-Brown Commission, *Preparing for the 21st Century: An Appraisal of U.S. Intelligence* (Washington DC, GPO, 1 March 1996), 87.

ogy supports, and is not a replacement for, the mental processes of analysis, highlights this opportunity.

However, it remains to be seen whether the agencies and their personnel are willing and able to carry out this essential work. Organizational changes now underway may not go far enough. Agency structures remain large and centrally planned. More agile responses to intelligence challenges, as yet undefined, may be required to counter them.[90]

A Community strategy focusing both on what consumers require, and how a professional analytic workforce can be developed is a logical follow-on to the transformations the Intelligence Community already has begun. The results of implementing such a strategy will be profound, if the transformations remain grounded in mission and are sustained through changes in leadership. In this climate, talented and motivated analysts who are highly knowledgeable about their consumers and their targets will apply rigorous analytic techniques to create actionable intelligence for decisionmakers. Under expert management, analysts will apply critical thinking skills in evaluating their own work, ensuring that it is of the highest caliber. As these analysts collaborate extensively across the Intelligence Community, the example they set will inspire others to excellence. Making this vision a reality requires action. The ideas developed here can be used as a guide to action and an instrument of change.

BIBLIOGRAPHY

Ackerman, Robert K. "Information Age Poses New Challenges to Intelligence." *Signal* 53, no. 2 (October 1998): 23-25.

Aid, Mathew M. "The Time of Troubles: The US National Security Agency in the Twenty-First Century." *Intelligence and National Security* 15, no. 3 (Autumn 2000): 1-32.

The American Heritage Dictionary, 2nd College Edition, 1976.

Aspin-Brown Commission. *Preparing for the 21st Century*. U.S. Congress. Senate. 103rd Cong., 2d sess. 1 March 1996.

Berkowitz, Bruce D. and Allan E. Goodman. *Best Truth: Intelligence in the Information Age*. New Haven, CT: Yale University Press, 2000.

_____. *Strategic Intelligence for American National Security*. Princeton, NJ: Princeton University Press, 1989.

Bozeman, Adda. *Politics and Culture in International History: From the Ancient Near East to the Opening of the Modern Age*, 2nd Edition. New Brunswick, NJ: Transaction Publishers, 1994.

---

[90] For an examination of how intelligence analysis might be done in the 21st Century, see chapter 4 of Bruce D. Berkowitz and Allan E. Goodman, *Best Truth: Intelligence in the Information Age* (New Haven: Yale University Press, 2000).

_____. *Strategic Intelligence and Statecraft: Selected Essays*. McLean, VA: Brassey's, 1992.

Brei, William S., Captain, USAF. *Getting Intelligence Right: The Power of Logical Procedure*. Occasional Paper Number Two. Washington DC: Joint Military Intelligence College, 1996.

Brown, John Seely and Paul Duguid. *The Social Life of Information*. (Boston, MA: Harvard Business School Press, 2000.

Bush, George W. "National Security Presidential Directive 5." 9 May 2001.

Christopher, Warren. *In the Stream of History: Shaping Foreign Policy for a New Era*. Stanford, CA: Stanford University Press, 1998.

Clauser, Jerome K. and Sandra M. Weir. *Intelligence Research Methodologies, An Introduction to Techniques and Procedures for Conducting Research in Defense Intelligence*. Washington DC: Defense Intelligence School, 1975.

Council on Foreign Relations. *Making Intelligence Smarter: The Future of U.S. Intelligence: A Report of an Independent Task Force*, n.d., n.p. Available from the Federation of American Scientists, <http://www.fas.org/irp/efr.html>. Last accessed 4 June 2001.

Deacon Terence W. T*he Symbolic Species: The co-Evolution of Language and the Brain* London: W.W. Norton & Company, Ltd., 1997.

Denning, Stephen. *The Springboard: How Storytelling Ignites Action in Knowledge-Era Organizations*. Boston, MA: Butterworth Heineman, 2001.

Devlin, Keith. "The Role of Conceptual Structure in Human Evolution." In Bernhard Ganter and Guy W. Mineau, eds. *Conceptual Structures: Logical, Linguistic, and Computational Issues*, Proceedings of the 8th International Conference on Conceptual Structures. Berlin, Germany: Springier Verlag, 2000.

Director of Central Intelligence, National Security Advisory Panel. *Strategic Investment Plan for Intelligence Community Analysis*. Washington DC: Central Intelligence Agency, 2000. URL: *<www.cia.gov/cia/publications/unclass_sip/index.html>*. Last accessed 1 July 2001.

Ember, Carol R. and Melvin Ember. *Anthropology*, 9th Edition. Upper Saddle River, NJ: Prentice Hall, 1999.

Folker, Robert D. Jr., MSgt. USAF. *Intelligence Analysis in Theater Joint Intelligence Centers: An Experiment in Applying Structured Methods*. Occasional Paper Number Seven. Washington DC: Joint Military Intelligence College, 2000.

Foster, Gregory D. "Research, Writing, and the Mind of the Strategist." *Joint Force Quarterly*, 11 (Spring 1996): 74-79.

Fuld, Leonard. "Intelligence Software: Reality or Still Virtual Reality." *Competitive Intelligence Magazine* 4, no. 2 (March-April 2001): 24-25.

Garst, Ronald D. and Max L. Gross. "On Becoming an Intelligence Analyst. *"Defense Intelligence Journal* 6, no. 2 (Fall 1997): 47-60.

Haxton, Brooks, tr. *Fragments, the Collected Wisdom of Heraclitus*. New York: Penguin, 2001.

Herring, Jan P. *Measuring the Effectiveness of Competitive Intelligence: Assessing and Communicating CI's Value to Your Organization*. Alexandria, VA: Society of Competitive Intelligence Professionals, 1996.

Heuer, Richards. *The Psychology of Intelligence Analysis*. Washington, DC: Center for the Study of Intelligence, 1999.

Huo, Zhongwen and Zongxiao Wang. *Guofang Keji Qingbaoyuan ji Houqu Jishu*) Sources and Techniques of Obtaining National Defense Science and Technology Intelligence). Beijing: Kexue Jishu Wenxuan Publishing Co., 1991.

Johnson, Loch K. "Analysis for a New Age." *Intelligence and National Security* 11, no. 4 (October 1996): 657-671.

_____. *Bombs, Bugs, Drugs, and Thugs: Intelligence and America's Quest for Security*. New York: New York University Press, 2000.

Juergensmeyer, Mark. *Terror in the Mind of God: the Global Rise of Religious Violence*. Berkeley: University of California Press, 2000.

Kalb, Clifford C. "Core Competencies: A Practitioner's View," document 207612, Merck & Co., Inc, n.d.

Kaplan, Robert D. *The Coming Anarchy: Shattering the Dreams of the Post-Cold War*. New York: Random House, 2000.

_____. *Eastward to Tartary: Travels in the Balkans, Middle East, and the Caucasus*. New York: Random House, 2000.

Kent, Sherman. "The Need for an Intelligence Literature," *Studies in Intelligence*, Spring, 1955. Reprinted in *Studies in Intelligence*, 45th Anniversary Special Edition, Washington DC: Government Printing Office, 2001, 1-11.

_____. *Strategic Intelligence for American World Policy*. Princeton, NJ: Princeton University Press, 1949.

Kovacs, Amos. "Using Intelligence." *Intelligence and National Security* 12, no. 4 (October 1997): 145-164.

Krizan, Lisa. *Intelligence Essentials for Everyone*. Occasional Paper Number 6. Washington DC: Joint Military Intelligence College, 1999.

Lorenz, Frederick M. and Edward J. Erickson. *The Euphrates Triangle: Security Implications of the Southeastern Anatolia Project*. Washington, DC: National Defense University Press, 1999.

Lowenthal, Mark M. *Intelligence: From Secrets to Policy*. Washington, DC: CQ Press, 2000.

Mann, Steven R. "Chaos Theory and Strategic Thought." *Parameters* 22, no. 3 (Autumn 1992): 54-68.

McDowell, Don. *Strategic Intelligence: A Handbook for Practitioners, Managers, and Users*. Cooma, Australia: Istana Enterprises, Pty. Ltd., 1998.

Mathams, R. H. "The Intelligence Analyst's Notebook," in *Strategic Intelligence: Theory and Application*, 2d. ed., Washington, DC: Joint Military Intelligence Training Center, 1995, 77-96.

National Drug Intelligence Center. *Basic Intelligence Analysis Course*, slide # 9. Power-Point Presentation, April 2001.

National Intelligence Council. *Global Trends 2015: A Dialogue About the Future with Nongovernment Experts*. Washington DC: National Foreign Intelligence Board, 2000.

National Security Agency External Team. *Report: A management Review for the Director, NSA*, 22 October 1999. URL: <*www.nsa.gov/releases/nsa_external_team_report.pdf*> Last accessed 4 June 2001.

Oxford Concise English-Chinese/Chinese-English Dictionary, 2nd ed. Oxford: Oxford U University Press, 1999.

Stack Kevin P. "Competitive Intelligence." *Intelligence and National Security* 13, no.4 (Winter 1998): 194-202.

Starbuck, William H. "Unlearning Ineffective or Obsolete Technologies." *International Journal of Technology Management* 11, nos. 7/8 (Winter 1996): 725-726.

Steele, Robert David. "The New Craft of Intelligence: an Alternative Approach Oriented to the Public," Paper presented at the 1st conference on the Future of Intelligence in the 21st Century, Priverno, Italy, 14-16 February 2001.

Steury, Donald P., ed. *Sherman Kent and the Board of National Estimates: Collected Essays*. Washington DC: Center for the Study of Intelligence, Central Intelligence Agency, 1994.

Swenson, Russell G., Francis J. Hughes, and others. "Research Design," in *Research: Design and Methods*. Ed. Russell G. Swenson. Washington DC: Joint Military Intelligence College, September 2000.

Treverton, Gregory. *Reshaping National Intelligence for an Age of Information*. Cambridge: Cambridge University Press, 2001.

Wheaton, Kristan J., *The Warning Solution: Intelligent Analysis in the Age of Information Overload*. Fairfax, VA: AFCEA International Press, 2001.

Williams, Phil and Roy Godson. "Anticipating Organized and Transnational Crime." Paper presented at the 1st conference on the Future of Intelligence in the 21st Century, Priverno, Italy, 14-16 February 2001.

Yu, Chong Ho. "Abduction? Deduction? Induction? Is there a Logic of Exploratory Data Analysis?" Paper presented at the annual meeting of the American Educational Research Association, New Orleans, LA, April 1994. URL: <http://seamonkey.ed.asu.edu/~behrens/asu/reports/Peirce/ Logic_of_EDA.html>. Last accessed 6 June 2001.

ABOUT THE AUTHOR

LT Michael Bennett enlisted in the Coast Guard in 1991. From 1991 to 1994 he was stationed at Marine Safety Office, Houston, Texas where he responded to oil and chemical spills and served as a member of a U.S. Customs Assist Team and Boarding Team Member enforcing federal laws and regulations in the Port of Houston/Upper Galveston Bay area. From 1994 to 1998, he was stationed at Marine Safety Office St. Louis, Missouri where he worked in the Port Operations Department responding to oil and chemical spills, enforcing federal environmental regulations and acting as the Safety and Occupational Health Coordinator for the Marine Safety Office and its two detachments located in Davenport, Iowa and St. Paul, Minnesota. In 1998, he received a Direct Commission as a Lieutenant Junior Grade and was assigned to the Office of Response at Coast Guard Headquarters where he assisted with the national and international coordination of the Coast Guard's Pollution Response Program and acted as the Coast Guard representative on the U.S. National Response Team, Response Sub-Committee. Prior to attending the Joint Military Intelligence College in 2002, LT Bennett was stationed at Marine Safety Office/Group Portland, Oregon where he was Assistant Chief of Contingency Preparedness and Planning, responsible for coordinating regional efforts relating to National Security, Port Security, Environmental Response, Anti-Terrorism and Force Protection, and response to Natural Disasters for the Pacific Northwest

THE U.S. COAST GUARD JOINS THE INTELLIGENCE COMMUNITY

Michael E. Bennett, LT, USCG

The United States Coast Guard (USCG), like many other agencies, has experienced significant transformation since 11 September 2001. For example, the evolution of the intelligence function in the USCG was dramatically hastened, resulting in its gaining full membership in the Intelligence Community by year's end. The multiple responsibilities of this service are focused on National Defense, Environmental Protection, and Maritime Safety, Security, and Mobility in protecting the expansive U.S. Maritime Transportation System (MTS), which extends over 95,000 miles of coastline, 360 seaports, and 3.4 million square miles of Exclusive Economic Zone (EEZ)[1]

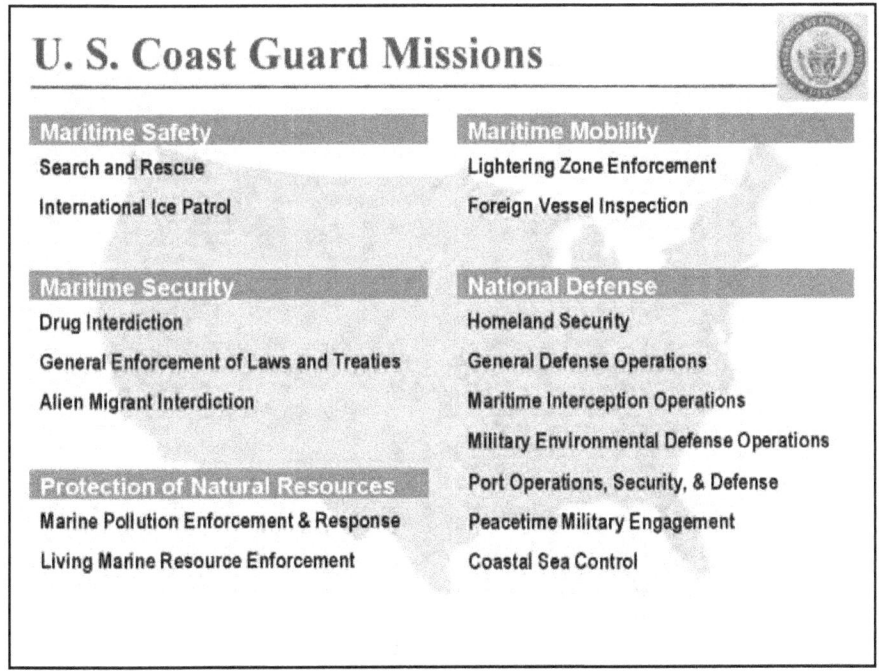

U. S. Coast Guard Missions

Maritime Safety
Search and Rescue
International Ice Patrol

Maritime Security
Drug Interdiction
General Enforcement of Laws and Treaties
Alien Migrant Interdiction

Protection of Natural Resources
Marine Pollution Enforcement & Response
Living Marine Resource Enforcement

Maritime Mobility
Lightering Zone Enforcement
Foreign Vessel Inspection

National Defense
Homeland Security
General Defense Operations
Maritime Interception Operations
Military Environmental Defense Operations
Port Operations, Security, & Defense
Peacetime Military Engagement
Coastal Sea Control

Source: Vice Admiral Allen, USCG, 7 October 2002.

---

[1] The EEZ consists of those areas adjoining the territorial sea of the U.S., the Commonwealth of Puerto Rico, the Commonwealth of the Northern Mariana Islands, and U.S. overseas territories and possessions. The EEZ extends up to 200 nautical miles from the U.S. coastline. The U.S. has sovereign rights over all living and non-living resources in the EEZ. Other nations may exercise freedom of vessel navigation and overflight within the EEZ. See *http://www.uscg.mil/hq/g-cp/com-rel/factfile/Factcards/ Homeland.htm* for a description of the USCG Maritime Homeland Security Strategy.

Historically Coast Guard Intelligence has focused on the collection of information in support of law enforcement operations related to counter-drug and migrant interdiction. With the migration to the Department of Homeland Security (DHS) and membership in the IC, a less sharp line now exists between National Foreign Intelligence and Law Enforcement Intelligence collection because of the need for both to anticipate and prosecute illegal international migration, piracy, and other transnational threats. The USCG is the only organization simultaneously responsible for law enforcement, intelligence, and military activities. Title 14 of the U.S. Code provides the Coast Guard with its Law Enforcement and Civil authorities, and Title 10 provides this service with National Defense and Military authorities. The figure below depicts the law enforcement/military continuum for these authorities and demonstrates the placement of USCG intelligence as a bridge between the realms of law enforcement and national foreign intelligence.

Coast Guard Civil/Military Authorities Source: Vice Admiral Allen, USCG, 7 October 2002.

THE COAST GUARD ROLE IN INTELLIGENCE

The roots of the Coast Guard intelligence function trace back to the Rum War during the period of prohibition. From 1920 to 1933, the USCG provided operational intelligence for law enforcement efforts.[2] After that era, although the Coast Guard continue intelligence support to its many law enforcement missions, not until 1984 did it establish the Intelligence Coordination Center (ICC), an information fusion activity that provides maritime intelligence support to the National Foreign Intelligence Community and Coast Guard commands at the strategic, operational and tactical level. In December 2001, through an amendment to the *National Security Act of 1947*, the USCG officially became a member of the Intelligence Community.[3] This development significantly expands the service's intelligence roles and responsibilities with respect to other members.

In a Congressional Research Service Report for Congress, a CIA official is cited as the source for the following observation comparing law enforcement and national security intelligence:

> Today there is no clear primacy for either the law enforcement or intelligence communities in the realms of international terrorism, narcotics, proliferation (as well as some areas of counterintelligence). Still, the law enforcement and intelligence communities remain designed to operate in fundamentally dissimilar manners, retaining different legal authorities, internal modes of organization and governing paradigms.[4]

As an organization straddling the boundaries between the law enforcement and intelligence communities, the USCG allows for collection of information domestically and abroad leading to detection, preemption and deterrence of threats, and when necessary, operations involving crisis and consequence management, and arrest and prosecution in the maritime environment.

ON BECOMING A COMMUNITY MEMBER

Community membership is a win-win for the Coast Guard and the Intelligence Community (IC). The IC gets a multi-mission agency with numerous regional, national, and international relationships, combined with extensive law enforcement and military authorities. The Coast Guard receives recognition for their existing efforts in support of national collection requirements, a clearly defined mission from the Director of Central Intelligence (DCI), and increased resources to support these new mission requirements.

---

[2] Robert E. Johnson, *Guardians of the Sea: History of the United States Coast Guard 1915 to the Present* (Annapolis, MD: Naval Institute Press, 1987), 89. Also see Eric S. Ensign, LT, USCG, *Intelligence in the Rum War at Sea*, 1920-1933 (Washington, DC: Joint Military Intelligence College, 2001).

[3] U.S. Congress, Senate, Intelligence Authorization Act for Fiscal Year 2002, 107th Cong, 1st sess., 2001, H. Res. 288.

[4] Richard A. Best, "Intelligence and Law Enforcement: Countering Transnational Threats to the U.S.," *CRS Report for Congress* RL30252 (Washington, DC: Congressional Research Service, Library of Congress, 3 December 2001), 2.

But IC membership also involves congressional oversight, training and education, and the development of an infrastructure ready to accept these new duties. How is the Coast Guard handling this new responsibility?

An N2 for the Coast Guard

In October of 2002, the position of Assistant Commandant for Intelligence (G-C2) was created, elevating the office to a Directorate level within the Coast Guard organization. This position is held by Senior Executive Service Officer Mrs. Frances Fragos Townsend. Her position provides direct access to the Commandant of the Coast Guard, essentially filling both the N2 (Director of Intelligence) and Naval Security Group (NSG) roles for the Coast Guard. Additionally, Mrs. Townsend and the Commandant of the Coast Guard share the responsibility as the service's Senior Official of the Intelligence Community (SOIC), ensuring compliance with all community tasking and related oversight.

Mrs. Townsend, who came from the Justice Department's Office of Intelligence Policy Review, is responsible for a burgeoning Intelligence Directorate that could soon number more than 150 people at the headquarters level alone. This moves the Intelligence Directorate out of its longtime position under Coast Guard Operations, significantly expanding its responsibilities and expectations, one of them being the development of a career path to support the new mission.

Establishing a New Career Path

Prior to community membership, being a Coast Guard Intelligence Officer could have been detrimental to one's career. It was not that the job lacked excitement or qualified people; a recognized career path simply did not exist. An intelligence officer usually came from the operational (law enforcement) or marine safety (waterways management/environmental response) community, did one tour as an intelligence officer, and then went back to their specialty in order to improve chances for promotion. With the creation of G-C2, a formal career path now exists for enlisted and officers alike, supported by a rapidly developing training and education program.

A Direct Commission Program for Intelligence Officers seeks qualified enlisted or officer candidates from other services who are interested in a career with the Coast Guard, and who meet the prerequisites for commissioning (a Baccalaureate degree, combined with intelligence or law enforcement-related experience). Opportunities also exist for Officers to engage in post-graduate education at the Joint Military Intelligence College, where they can pursue an accredited Master of Science of Strategic Intelligence degree.

Bridging the Gap between Law Enforcement Information and National Foreign Intelligence Collection

Recent Coast Guard initiatives combined with current Coast Guard legal authorities have laid a foundation for the collection, fusion, and analysis of information in support of the IC and Department of Homeland Security. With IC membership comes an increase in responsibilities. The DCI will task the Coast Guard based on the new mission recently approved. Additionally, the USCG will continue to support other national collection requirements, but this will be done through its own Intelligence Coordination Center (ICC) and the development of newly created Maritime Intelligence Fusion Centers (MIFC) and Field Information Support Teams (FIST). The MIFC's are strategic fusion centers on the east and west coast that will collect, analyze and fuse information in support of national objectives, and the FIST will collect law enforcement intelligence at strategic economic and military ports throughout the country.

The USCG is also expanding its visibility in the Community through participation in numerous multi-agency operations. Although they have always participated in national and regional Joint Terrorism Task Force operations, recent initiatives also include additional participation with the Defense Intelligence Agency's Joint Intelligence Task Force-Combating Terrorism (JITF-CT), the U.S. Northern Command, and the Central Intelligence Agency's Crime and Narcotics Center (CNC) and Crime and Terrorism Center (CTC).

Dealing with Congressional Oversight

With Community membership comes Congressional oversight, and for the Coast Guard this means clearly defining the separation between law enforcement and Intelligence Community duties by establishing policies and procedures for collection and management of information within the service. In order to provide the necessary separation between these elements and yet maintain the continuity needed for detection, pre-emption and deterrence of threats, the Coast Guard has worked closely with the Community Management Staff and other intelligence organizations to capture best practices and lessons learned in order to avoid the information-sharing pitfalls experienced by other agencies. These lessons learned were then incorporated into the *Coast Guard Intelligence Capstone Document*[5] that delineates the role of the Coast Guard Intelligence Organization. The *Capstone Document* describes the Coast Guard Intelligence Program as a "binary organization consisting of two closely linked parts: the *National Intelligence Element* and the *Law Enforcement Intelligence Program.*"

---

[5] United States Coast Guard, *Coast Guard Capstone Document, COMDTINST 3820.10*, 26 February 2003 (Washington D.C.). Cited hereafter as Capstone Document.

The *National Intelligence Element* conducts "intelligence activities," as described in Executive Order 12333 and the National Security Act of 1947, including the collection, retention, and dissemination, of *national intelligence (foreign intelligence and counter-intelligence)* under those authorities. The National Intelligence Element is part of the Intelligence Community and is governed by procedures approved by the Attorney General. The National Intelligence Element consists of only those personnel or components designated by the Assistant Commandant for Intelligence, with the approval of the Chief of Staff.

The *Law Enforcement Intelligence Program* describes the collection, retention, and dissemination of information pursuant to Coast Guard law enforcement and regulatory authority. Persons and components that collect, process and report law enforcement intelligence and other information, including those persons performing intelligence functions as a collateral duty, are conducting functions under the Law Enforcement Intelligence Program. These persons and components are not part of the National Intelligence Element.[6]

Additionally, under provisions of the USA PATRIOT ACT and *Homeland Security Act of 2002* (HLS), the Coast Guard (in addition to other agencies) is required to provide critical information or intelligence, "gathered in the course of operations to enforce criminal laws," to the DCI. Warning information on foreign or terrorist threats is also reported to the Undersecretary for Information Analysis and Infrastructure Protection in the Department of Homeland Security as required under the Homeland Security Act of 2002. Foreign Intelligence is defined in the *National Security Act of 1947* as "information related to the capabilities, intentions, or activities of foreign governments, foreign organizations, foreign persons, or international terrorist activities" related to threats against the United States."[7] These provisions are designed to eliminate obstacles for sharing law enforcement information with the DCI while enhancing the ability of DHS to "connect the dots between diffuse bits of information"[8] in order to detect and preempt terrorist activities. Prior to 11 September 2001 there was no one agency responsible for coordinating this task throughout the federal government. In the Coast Guard this responsibility for reporting rests with G-C2. By centralizing the reporting of this information within one directorate, the Coast Guard will be able to reduce circular and duplicate reporting and simultaneously measure the effectiveness of Coast Guard information sharing practices.[9]

---

[6] Capstone Document, Enclosure 1.

[7] United States Coast Guard, "Implementation of Mandatory Information Sharing Provisions Under the USA PATRIOT ACT and Homeland Security Act of 2002," *Memorandum*, (Washington D.C.): 23 January 2003. Cited hereafter as USCG Memorandum.

[8] Richard A. Best, "Homeland Security: Intelligence Support," *CRS Report for Congress* RS21283 (Washington, DC: Congressional Research Service, Library of Congress, 4 March 2003).

[9] USCG Memorandum.

By circumscribing the relationships between the *National Intelligence Element* and *Law Enforcement Intelligence Program*, as approved by the Attorney General, the Coast Guard remains the only federal agency that is simultaneously a law enforcement, military, and intelligence service. Having this capability within the newly created Department of Homeland Security, Secretary Ridge now has a powerful tool: the ability to collect, analyze, and fuse law enforcement intelligence with national foreign intelligence that can lead to the critical pre-emption of transnational or asymmetric threats to homeland security or to interests abroad. As noted by one senior Coast Guard Intelligence official: "The different designations of *Law Enforcement Intelligence* and *National Intelligence* defines how information is collected and not how it is used."[10]

Avoiding the Pitfalls

A CRS report for Congress has noted that several pitfalls appear "systemic" in the Intelligence Community: "lack of preparedness to deal with challenges of global terrorism, inefficiencies in budgetary planning, the lack of adequate numbers of linguists, a lack of human sources, and an unwillingness to share information among agencies."[11] Although new to the IC, the Coast Guard is not unversed in some or even all of these problems. One aspect where the Coast Guard has considerable experience is in sharing information with other agencies. As a small agency with limited resources and far-reaching responsibilities, the Coast Guard has developed extensive partnerships at the federal, state, and local level in order to accomplish its mission. Most, if not all Coast Guard operations involve multi-agency and interagency cooperation. However, one aspect needing further attention by the service is its lack of a formal language-training program. While the Coast Guard does have linguists, very few have attended a formal language school, and even fewer have the requisite skills necessary to meet the standards required of its Defense Department counterparts.

An October 1996 article presaged the difficulties facing a new intelligence organization. It notes that "launching and maintaining an intelligence system is a complex task. The hardest part is achieving the right level of balance among the key system elements, especially among published information, human collection, and analysis."[12] In other agencies, the organizational culture and information-sharing practices have often limited the flow and accuracy of information between the analyst and the decisionmaker. As Lowenthal observes, "a dialogue between producers and consumers should take place after the intelligence has been received. Policymakers should give the intelligence community some sense of how well their requirements are

---

[10] Senior Intelligence Official, at the U.S. Coast Guard Office of Intelligence, interviewed by the author, 12 March 2003.

[11] Richard A. Best, "Intelligence Issues for Congress," Issue Brief for Congress IB 10012 (Washington, DC: Congressional Research Service, Library of Congress, Updated 6 March 2003), 14.

[12] "Intelligence Pitfalls," *Management Review*, 85, no. 10 (October 1996): 51.

being met and discuss any adjustments needed"[13] Clearly defined requirements combined with doctrine, process, and training and education are the key, systematic elements that can provide the necessary balance the Coast Guard needs as a successful member of the IC.

As Amy Zegart concludes, "to do their jobs, national security officials must concern themselves with other agencies...their activities inherently overlap and intersect."[14] A noteworthy benefit of Coast Guard membership in the IC is that the service has no culture of "owning" information. On the contrary, the service has a reputation for sharing information (while maintaining the necessary safety protections) leading to relationship-building that can provide enhanced detection, pre-emption, and deterrence, while bringing together civilian, law enforcement, intelligence, and military agencies to combat threats to the homeland. These combined responsibilities to collect, analyze, and fuse law enforcement and national foreign intelligence information rest with an agency that has historically had a reputation for public trust and confidence.

---

[13] Mark M. Lowenthal, *Intelligence: From Secrets to Policy, 2d* rev ed. (Washington D.C.: CQ Press, 2003) 42.

[14] Amy B. Zegart, *Flawed by Design: The Evolution of the CIA, JCS and NSC* (California: Stanford University Press, 1999), 37.

INDEX

A

C

D

E

F

H

I

Other Books from the Joint Military Intelligence College

Pickert, Perry L. *Intelligence for Multilateral Decision and Action*, 1997.

Clift, A. Denis. *Clift Notes*. James S. Major, ed., 2000.

Ensign, Eric S., LT, USCG. *Intelligence in the Rum War at Sea*, 1920-1933, 2001.

Clift, A. Denis. *Clift Notes*, 2nd Ed. James S. Major, ed., 2002.

Grabo, Cynthia M. *Anticipating Surprise: Analysis for Strategic Warning*. Jan Goldman, ed., 2002.

Bringing Intelligence About: Practitioners Reflect on Best Practices. Russell G. Swenson, ed., 2003.